FEARON'S

Basic English

SECOND EDITION

FEARON'S

Basic English

SECOND EDITION

Joan Kreisl

GLOBE FEARON
EDUCATIONAL PUBLISHER
PARAMUS, NEW JERSEY

Paramount Publishing

Pacemaker Curriculum Advisor: Stephen C. Larsen

Stephen C. Larsen holds a B.S. and an M.S. in Speech Pathology from the University of Nebraska at Omaha, and an Ed.D. in Learning Disabilities from the University of Kansas. In the course of his career, Dr. Larsen has worked in the Teacher Corps on a Nebraska Indian Reservation, as a Fullbright senior lecturer in Portugal and Spain, and as a speech pathologist in the public schools. A full professor at the University of Texas at Austin, he has nearly twenty years' experience as a teacher trainer on the university level. He is the author of sixty journal articles, three textbooks and six widely used standardized tests including the Test of Written Learning (TOWL) and the Test of Adolescent Language (TOAL).

Subject Area Consultants: M.B. Clarke and A.G. Clarke

Both M.B. Clarke and A.G. Clarke earned Ph.D.s in English at the University of California, Berkeley. Together they have developed composition and reading materials for a wide range of educational publishers. Both also score national writing tests for the Educational Testing Service. M.B. Clarke teaches composition at the University of California, Davis, and A.G. Clarke teaches writing in the University of California, Berkeley, Extension Freshman Program and at Sacramento City College.

Editors: Stephen Feinstein and Karen Bernhaut

Editorial Assistant: Stacie Dozier

Text Designer: Dianne Platner

Art Director: Nancy Sharkey

Production Manager: Penny Gibson

Production Editor: Nicole Cypher

Desktop Specialist: Eric Dawson

Manufacturing Supervisor: Della Smith

Cover Design: Mark Ong, Side by Side Studios

Cover photo: Nick Gunderson/AllStock

Other photos: Rob Crandall/Stock Boston 108; Michael Dwyer/Stock Boston 42; Gerard Fritz/Jeroboam, Inc. 198; Judy S. Gelles/Stock Boston 2; John Herr 56, 130, 146, 242; Robert A. Isaacs 78, 164; Frank Keillor/Jeroboam, Inc. 16, 94; Oregon State Highway Department 226; Squibb Laboratories 210; Peter Vandermark/Stock Boston 180.

Printed in the United States of America   3 4 5 6 7 8 9 10 99 98 97 96

ISBN 835-91038-5

GLOBE FEARON
EDUCATIONAL PUBLISHER
PARAMUS, NEW JERSEY

Paramount Publishing

A Note to the Student

Some things that seem hard at first turn out to be easy. Remember when you first tried to ride a bicycle? You didn't get very far until you learned to balance, pedal, and steer. You probably made mistakes and fell down at first. But all it took was a little practice to get you going. Then you could take off in any direction you wanted to. The world was yours!

Studying language is a lot like learning to ride a bicycle. Until you learn the basics, you can't get very far. But all it takes is some practice to get you going. Then, like a bicycle, your basic language skills will speed you along wherever you want to go.

The purpose of this book is to make it easier for you to succeed at school, at work, and in the outside world. Chapter by chapter, you will learn about nouns, pronouns, verbs, and other parts of speech. And you will learn about different kinds of sentences and how sentences are put together. Perhaps you will never have to identify an adverb or a predicate again. But it is still important to learn these English basics. They are the building blocks of our language. Once you know how words and sentences work, you won't even have to think about it. Like pedaling and balancing, this understanding will become automatic. It will help you every time you write a letter, give a set of directions, or prepare a report.

All through the book you'll find notes in the margins of the pages. These friendly notes are there to make you stop and think. Sometimes they comment on the material you're learning. Sometimes they give examples, and sometimes they remind you of something you already know.

Watch for the study aids throughout the book. At the beginning of every chapter, you'll find **learning objectives**. These will help you focus on the important points covered in the chapter. And you'll find **Words to Know**, a look ahead at the vocabulary you may find difficult. At the end of each chapter, a **summary** will give you a quick review of what you've just learned.

Everyone who put this book together worked hard to make it useful, interesting, and enjoyable. The rest is up to you. We wish you well in your studies. Our success is in your accomplishment.

Unit One

Sentences
and
Punctuation

Chapter 1

Parts of the Sentence

*The people in the photograph are speaking to each other.
Without even thinking about it, they are using sentences.
Grouping words in sentences helps us to organize facts,
ideas, and feelings. We use sentences to communicate with
each other.*

Chapter Learning Objectives

Define a sentence.

Use capital letters in sentences.

Name the four kinds of sentences.

Identify subjects and predicates in sentences.

Use end punctuation in sentences.

Use sentences in speaking and writing.

Words to Know

declarative sentence a sentence that tells what someone or something is or does

exclamatory sentence a sentence that shows strong feeling

imperative sentence a sentence that gives a command or makes a request

interrogative sentence a sentence that asks a question

predicate the part of the sentence that tells what the subject does or is

sentence a group of words that expresses a complete thought

subject the part of the sentence that tells who or what the sentence is about

Lesson 1: What Is a Sentence?

A **sentence** is a group of words that expresses a complete thought.

☐ These are sentences.

> The dogs ate his food.

> The cat stole some food.

☐ These are not sentences.

> The dogs.

This group of words does not tell what the dogs did.

> Stole some food.

This group of words does not tell who stole some food.

Practice 1

Some of the groups of words below are sentences. Some are not. Copy only the sentences on a separate sheet of paper.

1. The man had suddenly disappeared.
2. At the end of a long horror movie.
3. Remembered my name.
4. Helen leaped over the hurdle easily.
5. The winner was Sheila.

Lesson 2: Kinds of Sentences

There are four kinds of sentences.

☐ A **declarative sentence** tells something. It ends with a period.

> Our team won the game.

☐ An **interrogative sentence** asks a question. It ends with a question mark.

> Who won the game?

You use sentences all the time! That's how you communicate. What was the last thing you said to another person? How many sentences did you use?

☐ An **imperative sentence** makes a request or gives a command. It ends with a period or an exclamation point.

> Please buy tickets for the next game.

> Get out of my way!

☐ An **exclamatory sentence** shows strong feeling. It ends with an exclamation point.

> That was the best game of the season!

Practice 1

Number a separate sheet of paper from 1 to 10. Next to the number for each sentence, write a letter to show what kind of sentence it is. Write **D** for declarative, **In** for interrogative, **Im** for imperative, and **E** for exclamatory. The first one is done for you.

1. Who plays shortstop on that baseball team?

   In

2. He graduated from Disco Tech.

3. Just sign the check over to me.

4. What kind of an animal is that?

5. It's turning orange!

6. How many teeth does a shark have?

7. What a silly suggestion that was!

8. Iowa got its name from an Indian word meaning "sleepy ones."

9. Please count them again.

10. Do you think you could carry a million one-dollar bills?

Lesson 3: Subjects and Predicates in Declarative Sentences

Every sentence has two main parts: a **subject** and a **predicate**.

☐ The subject tells who or what the sentence is about. In most declarative sentences, the subject is the first part of the sentence.

   People came to see the caves.

   Three new guides showed the visitors around.

☐ The predicate tells what the subject does or is. In most declarative sentences, the predicate is the second part of the sentence.

The group **entered the cave slowly**.

Everyone **looked around**.

Practice 1

On a separate sheet of paper, copy each sentence. Draw one line under the subject. Draw two lines under the predicate. The first one is done for you.

1. Roger writes to me often.

   Roger writes to me often.

2. They went to every football game last year.

3. A messenger will deliver the package tomorrow.

4. Donna and he make scented candles.

5. Lobsters have five pairs of legs.

6. Banks and many businesses will close for the holiday.

7. Nobody wanted to spoil the surprise.

8. Benjamin Franklin was a statesman, a printer, a writer, and a scientist.

Practice 2

Write these subjects on a separate sheet of paper. Then add a predicate to each one. The first one is done for you.

1. Those rusty scissors _____ .

   Those rusty scissors are on the table.

2. The most experienced detectives in the department _____ .

3. A track of muddy footprints _____ .

4. Most football coaches _____ .

5. No one else in the whole town _____ .

In a few declarative sentences, the predicate is the first part. The subject is the second part.

In the sentences below, the predicate is in dark type. Notice where it appears in each sentence.

The girl **ran down the street.**

Down the street ran the girl.

Words
to the Wise

The early bird gets the worm.

Have you ever heard anyone say this? A proverb is an old and well-known saying that states a truth or gives advice. For thousands of years people all over the world have used proverbs to share their wisdom.

Write this proverb on a separate sheet of paper. Draw one line under the subject and two lines under the predicate. Then think about what message this proverb has for people. Remember: proverbs are always about **people**. This proverb, for example, isn't really talking about birds and worms. Explain what this proverb means in your own words.

Practice 3

On a separate sheet of paper, write the predicates from these sentences. The first one is done for you.

1. Onto the scene rushed Eric and Jay.

   Onto the scene rushed

2. They set the box down near the chair.

3. From these seeds will spring new plants.

4. Ed and Gina danced quickly across the floor.

5. Across the lawn rolled an old tennis ball.

6. Bob was relaxing on the couch.

7. Under the couch lay Rebecca's missing book.

8. Out of the faucet dripped three drops of water.

9. Near the chair sat a yawning cat.

10. Toward her drifted the smell of sardine sandwiches.

Practice 4

Write five different sentences on a separate sheet of paper. Use the subjects and predicates in the boxes.

Kim and Andy	were inside the box.
We	were looking for food.
Some heavy things	ring loudly and clearly.
The bells	sat under the pine tree.
Bears	fell from the shelf.

Challenge

Write a sentence with the predicate first. Use a subject and a predicate from the boxes in Practice 4. You will need to change the order of the words in the predicate.

Lesson 4: Subjects and Predicates in Interrogative Sentences

Every interrogative sentence has a subject and a predicate.

In some interrogative sentences the subject is the first part and the predicate is the second part.

Notice the subjects in dark type.

> **Who** came first?

> **Which package** was largest?

Practice 1

Write the subjects from these interrogative sentences on a separate sheet of paper. The first one is done for you.

1. Which was the winning entry?

   Which

2. What will happen on Saturday?
3. Who will bring a green salad?
4. Whose gloves are missing?
5. Which one was the bargain?

Try this for fun!

Think of something you always wanted to ask your best friend. Either you never got around to it, or you were afraid to ask. Well, now's your chance! But you'll have to use an interrogative sentence.

In many interrogative sentences, part of the predicate comes before the subject.

Notice the predicate in dark type.

Why did the butler **lie about it?**

Here's how you can find the subject of this kind of interrogative sentence.

Step 1: Change the order of the words in the sentence. Now the sentence seems to be a declarative sentence. This sentence may sound a little strange. But it can help you find the subject and predicate.

Why did the butler lie about it?

The butler did lie about it why.

Step 2: Find the subject and predicate of the new sentence.

subject: The butler

predicate: did lie about it why.

The butler is the subject of the interrogative sentence.

Practice 2

Take out a separate sheet of paper. Rewrite each of the following interrogative sentences as if it were a declarative sentence. Decide what is the subject and what is the predicate. Draw one line under the subject. Draw two lines under the predicate. The first one is done for you.

1. Why do snakes shed their skins?

   Snakes do shed their skins why.

2. How did you find the correct answer?

3. When did Edith arrive?

4. What does the doctor recommend?

5. Where does that winding path lead?

6. How could Larry say such a thing?

7. At what time did she leave?

8. Can Jamie help you?

9. Does anyone have any idea?

10. Will it rain tomorrow?

Lesson 5: Subjects and Predicates in Imperative Sentences

In most imperative sentences only the predicate is written or spoken. The subject of the sentence is understood. That subject is always **you**.

Please speak to her tonight.

You must speak to her tonight!

Practice 1

Write the subjects of these sentences on a separate sheet of paper. If the subject is understood to be you, write **you**. The first one is done for you.

1. Go to Grand Boulevard and turn right.

   you

2. Where are they going on vacation?

3. Anything is possible.

4. Who knows the words to this song?

5. Barbara and Jose will organize the car wash.

6. Never speak to me that way again!

7. Yolanda is an excellent swimmer.

8. Why won't Mr. Mifune be there?

9. Tell me which movie you liked best.

10. You should always stop at a red light.

Imagine that you are a fire chief. A fire is burning out of control. The fire fighters are waiting for your commands. What will you say? Remember to use imperative sentences.

Lesson 6: Capital Letters and End Punctuation in Sentences

☐ Every sentence begins with a capital letter.
   The man was a stranger.

☐ Declarative sentences end with a period.
   He had just arrived in town.

☐ Interrogative sentences end with a question mark.
   Did he come on the bus?

☐ Imperative sentences end with a period or an exclamation point.

> Tell me about him. Tell me about him at once!

☐ Exclamatory sentences end with an exclamation point.

> How mysterious he seems!

Practice 1

Rewrite these sentences on a separate sheet of paper. Use capital letters and end punctuation. The first one is done for you.

1. for years Cory had wanted a car

   For years Cory had wanted a car.

2. how could he earn the money he needed

3. he found a job at the supermarket

4. it took a long time to save enough money

5. at last he had enough

6. where should he go to buy a car

7. he saw a red convertible at Square Deal Cars

8. the car was a dream

9. did he have enough money

10. to his surprise the car was very cheap

11. there was one problem

12. the engine would not start

13. did that discourage Cory

14. tell me

15. he decided to fix the car

Chapter Review

Chapter Summary

☐ A sentence is a group of words that expresses a complete thought. Every sentence begins with a capital letter.

Sentence: Floyd ice skates every winter.

Not a Sentence: Ice skating every winter.

☐ A declarative sentence tells what someone or something is or does. It ends with a period.

Declarative sentence: This is my new hat.

☐ An interrogative sentence asks a question. It ends with a question mark.

Interrogative sentence: Who owns that hat?

☐ An imperative sentence makes a request or gives a command. It can end with a period or an exclamation point.

Imperative sentences: Please tell me how to do that. Come quickly!

☐ An exclamatory sentence shows strong feeling. It ends with an exclamation point.

Exclamatory sentence: That's amazing!

☐ The subject of a sentence tells who or what the sentence is about.

Subject: Clara has three cats.

☐ The predicate of a sentence tells what the subject does or is.

Predicate: Clara's cats **love to climb trees.**

Chapter Quiz

A. Complete each sentence below. Use the correct word from the box. Rewrite the sentences on a separate sheet of paper.

subject	declarative	predicate
imperative	interrogative	exclamatory

1. An _____ sentence shows strong feeling.

2. A question mark is used with an _____ sentence.

3. The two main parts of a sentence are the _____ and the _____ .

4. The subject of an _____ sentence is always you.

B. Copy these sentences on a separate sheet of paper. Draw one line under the subject. Draw two lines under the predicate. If the subject is understood to be you, write **you** after the sentence.

1. What happened to you yesterday?

2. I was sick in bed.

3. Please don't cough near me.

4. We hate colds!

C. Rewrite these sentences on a separate sheet of paper. Use capital letters and the correct end punctuation. Then draw two lines under the predicate of each sentence.

1. jerry saw a strange sight last night

2. what could he see in the dark

3. tell us

4. something in the room was glowing

Chapter 2 Punctuation

Look at the person in the picture. She is seated at a desk writing. Perhaps she is writing a letter. She will be using punctuation in order to make the meaning of what she is writing clearer.

Chapter Learning Objectives

Use commas to clarify the meaning of a sentence.

Use commas in a series.

Identify words in a sentence that need to be set off with commas.

Use punctuation with direct quotations.

Use commas in dates and in place names.

Use commas or exclamation points with interjections.

Use colons, semicolons, and hyphens.

Words to Know

colon **:** a punctuation mark that is used to introduce a series of items

comma **,** a punctuation mark that indicates a short pause between words or groups of words

hyphen **-** a punctuation mark that is used between parts of compound numbers, fractions, and certain compound words

interjection a word that expresses emotion and that is followed by an exclamation point or a comma
examples: wow gee oh

quotation marks **" "** punctuation marks that are used to show the beginning and end of someone's exact words

semicolon **;** a punctuation mark that is used to show a stronger break in thought than that shown by a comma but less than that shown by a period

Lesson 1: Using Commas to Avoid Confusion in a Sentence

Punctuation marks are used to make writing easier to understand. These marks tell a reader where to pause or stop. In Chapter 1 you learned about different kinds of sentences. You learned that every sentence ends with either a period, a question mark, or an exclamation point. These punctuation marks tell you whether you are reading a statement, a question, or an exclamation. Without them, words would just go on and on. It would be very difficult to understand what somebody was trying to say.

I don't know why he is acting this way did he hear some good news no wonder he is so excited he won the lottery

I don't know why he is acting this way. Did he hear some good news? No wonder he is so excited. He won the lottery!

When you are speaking, it is often necessary to pause in the middle of a sentence. By doing this, you show that there is a break in your thought. You put words into groups. The same thing happens in writing. You put a **comma** in a sentence to indicate a pause. The comma divides a sentence into groups of words. This makes your writing clearer.

In the afternoon traffic filled the streets.

After returning my uncle had dinner.

Use a comma to make the meaning clearer.

In the afternoon, traffic filled the streets.

After returning, my uncle had dinner.

Practice 1

Rewrite each of these sentences on a separate sheet of paper. Use commas where they are needed in order to avoid confusion in the sentence. The first one has been done for you.

1. Under a pile of newspapers a mouse was hiding.

   Under a pile of newspapers, a mouse was hiding.

2. After he made his speech John did not say another word.

3. On the old desk Paul noticed a book.

4. After the storm was over the lights came on.

5. Whenever Mary went to the movies Bob went with her.

6. With those parting words she left.

7. What were they going to do with the books he wondered.

8. If you tell me when the show starts I will be there on time.

9. At the back of the room he had hidden her hat.

10. Remember to loan me your study notes because I lost mine.

Words to the Wise

Lie down with dogs, get up with fleas.

Write this proverb on a separate sheet of paper. Notice where the comma is placed. Read the sentence out loud. Did you pause after the word "dogs"? That's why the comma is there. Without the comma, the sentence would be confusing. You might think that the sentence is trying to say, "dogs get up with fleas."

Now think about what this saying means. Remember: proverbs are about people. This proverb isn't really talking about dogs and fleas. Explain the meaning of this old saying in your own words.

Lesson 2: Using Commas in a Series

In writing, three or more of the same kind of items in a row form a **series**. Each item can be a single word or a group of words. A comma is used after every item in a series except the last.

Gina saw **Terry, Kiko, Mitch,** and **Pam**.

Each student had to **answer three questions, draw a map,** and **write an essay**.

Practice 1

Rewrite each of these sentences on a separate sheet of paper. Use commas where they are needed to separate items. The first one has been done for you.

1. Carl Jed and Louis agreed to work harder.

   Carl, Jed, and Louis agreed to work harder.

2. Running swimming and skiing are his favorite sports.

3. Has anyone seen Cheryl Patricia or Kathy?

4. On his way west Jim drove through Texas New Mexico and Arizona.

5. When he looked out his window he saw flowers grass and trees.

6. Stan enjoys the music of Bach Beethoven and Brahms.

7. Why are Cadillacs Lincolns and Jaguars so expensive?

8. Ronald came home from school put away his books and ran outside to play.

9. The weather turned cold wet and windy last Friday.

10. Paul took out his camera loaded it with film and began taking pictures.

Practice 2

On a separate sheet of paper, use each of the following series in a sentence of your own. Use commas where necessary. Remember to use end punctuation. The first one has been done for you.

1. robins sparrows and blackbirds

   In the forest he could hear the sounds of robins, sparrows, and blackbirds.

2. trucks cars and busses

3. blue red and yellow

4. January February and March

5. put his key in the lock opened the door and went inside

6. looked at his watch threw on his coat and ran downstairs

7. New York Boston and Philadelphia

8. north south east and west

9. morning afternoon and evening

10. Larry Richard and Manny

Lesson 3: Using Commas to Set Off Words in a Sentence

Sometimes a sentence begins with an introductory word or group of words. In speaking, you would pause after the introductory word. In writing, use a comma to separate the introductory word or words from the rest of the sentence. This makes the meaning of the sentence clearer.

Yes, Jeff is going to New York.

Running home, I fell and ripped my pants.

You do not have to use a comma if there would be little or no pause in speaking.

At last the dinner was ready.

Sometimes a word or group of words interrupts the flow of thought in a sentence. Use commas to set off such a word or words from the rest of the sentence.

Norm is, I hope, going to help us.

His name, most likely, will never be forgotten.

A noun is usually the name of a person, place, or thing. You will learn more about nouns in Chapters 3 and 4.

When you speak to someone, you often use his or her name in a sentence. A name in such a sentence is called a **noun of address**. Use a comma after a noun of address at the beginning of a sentence.

Nick, can you help us?

Use a comma before a noun of address at the end of a sentence.

Can you help us, Nick?

If a noun of address comes in the middle of a sentence, use commas before and after the noun of address.

I'll be happy, Nan, to help you.

Practice 1

Rewrite each of these sentences on a separate sheet of paper. Use commas correctly with any nouns of address that you find. The first one has been done for you.

1. Beam me up Scotty!

   Beam me up, Scotty!

2. Well Bones what is your diagnosis?

3. Mr. Sulu go to Warp 5.

4. If it weren't for you Spock there'd be no aliens aboard.

5. Why do we have to wear these funny clothes Captain?

Practice 2

Remember: a comma in writing is like a pause in speaking.

Rewrite each of these sentences on a separate sheet of paper. Use commas wherever they are needed to set off a word or group of words from the rest of the sentence. The first one is done for you.

1. Mary's idea is I think the best one of all.

   Mary's idea is, I think, the best one of all.

2. Ms. Stevens I have a question.

3. This is a problem Gloria that we must solve together.

4. Hal I suppose is very popular with his teammates.

5. Running quickly Jim got to the door first.

6. Can you stop at the store for me Frank?

7. Dr. Solway our family doctor can probably help.

8. The answer it seems is simple.

9. Mel this call is for you.

10. No Judy will not read her report today.

Lesson 4: Using Punctuation Correctly with Direct Quotations

A direct quotation tells the exact words a person said. Use **quotation marks** at the beginning and end of a direct quotation. A comma is used to separate the words of the quotation from the words that tell who is speaking.

Watson said, "I'm not leaving town."

A quotation can be either **direct** or **indirect**. In an indirect quotation you change the words of a speaker or writer to your own words. No quotation marks or commas are used.

Watson said that he is not leaving.

Sometimes a direct quotation is divided into two parts. Use quotation marks at the beginning and end of each part of the quotation. Notice where the commas are placed.

"Holmes," cried Watson, "that's amazing!"

A direct quotation often comes at the end of a sentence. The end punctuation is placed inside the quotation marks if it belongs to the quotation.

Watson exclaimed, "She was on the train!"

Holmes asked, "Don't you see the importance of that?"

Watson replied, "No, I don't."

Commas and periods are placed inside the quotation marks at the end of a quotation. Other punctuation marks are placed outside the quotation marks unless they belong to the quotation.

> Did Holmes say, "That is important"?

Sometimes the direct quotation comes before the name of the speaker. If the quotation is a statement or command, use a comma at the end of it. If the quotation is a question, use a question mark. If the quotation is an exclamation, use an exclamation point.

> "The train did not arrive until eleven o'clock," said Holmes.

> "And the body was discovered at ten o'clock!" exclaimed Watson.

> "Now do you understand why the time was so important?" asked Holmes.

Practice 1

Rewrite these sentences on a separate sheet of paper. Use quotation marks with any direct quotations you find. The first one has been done for you.

1. Will Rogers said, I never met a man I didn't like.

   Will Rogers said, "I never met a man I didn't like."

2. All politics is applesauce, he also said.

3. Peel me a grape, Mae West said.

4. A tie, Bear Bryant claimed, is like kissing your sister.

5. I want to be alone, Greta Garbo said.

6. Knute Rockne told his team, Win one for the Gipper.

7. Here's looking at you, kid, Humphrey Bogart said.

8. He *didn't* say, Play it again, Sam.

9. The game's not over, Yogi Bera said, till it's over.

10. Oliver Twist said, Please, Sir, I want some more.

Practice 2

Rewrite each sentence on a separate sheet of paper. Use quotation marks, commas, periods, question marks, or exclamation points where they are needed. The first one has been done for you.

1. What should I do next asked Bradley.

   "What should I do next?" asked Bradley.

2. Which road goes to Taunton asked the stranger.

3. Jane replied Bradford Boulevard goes all the way.

4. A quicker way said Millie is to take West Street to Route 11.

5. Not now insisted Mike Road work is being done on West Street.

6. Where do you want to go in Taunton asked Jane.

7. The stranger replied The courthouse.

8. Then said Jane you should take Curtis Drive.

9. Thank you said the stranger I'll ask at the gas station.

10. Do you think he didn't trust our directions asked Mike.

Begin the first word in a direct quotation with a capital letter.

> Marian asked, "Where did the cat hide now?"

Sometimes the words that tell who is speaking divide a direct quotation into two parts. If the second part of the quotation is part of the sentence, do not begin it with a capital letter.

If the second part of the quotation is a new sentence, begin it with a capital letter.

> "Where," asked Marian, "did the cat hide now?"

> "I know where the cat is," said Fran. "Look over there."

Practice 3

Rewrite each sentence on a separate sheet of paper. Use capital letters where they are needed. The first one has been done for you.

1. Mark asked, "do you enjoy french food?"

   Mark asked, "Do you enjoy French food?"

2. Jack said, "across the street is a good restaurant."

3. "politeness," Emerson claimed, "ruins conversations."

4. "I see," said Tim, "that the mail has arrived."

5. "look over there!" Mary cried. "a tree fell down!"

6. "it all depends," said Sam, "on what they plan to do."

7. "The last time I was in New York," Ronald said, "it rained all week."

8. Herb said, "we better leave now or we'll be late."

9. "here comes the train," said Jane.

10. "Well," Sharon said, "the traffic is always bad around this time."

Lesson 5: Using Commas in Dates and in Place Names

Use a comma between the number of the day and the number of the year in a date.

> The last baseball triple-header was on October 2, 1920.

If the date does not come at the end of a sentence, put another comma after the end of the year.

> At the end of the day on October 2, 1920, many baseball fans were tired.

Do not use a comma in a date that has only the name of the month and the number of the year.

> We moved here in August 1982.

Practice 1

Rewrite these sentences on a separate sheet of paper. Use commas wherever they are needed. The first one has been done for you.

1. The first drive-in movie opened on June 6 1933.

   The first drive-in movie opened on June 6, 1933.

2. On March 2 1962 Wilt Chamberlain scored 100 points.

3. The first U.S. newspaper ad was published on May 1 1704.

4. August 18 1902 saw the first unassisted triple play.

5. Direct-dial long-distance calls began on October 10 1951.

6. On February 10 1933 the first singing telegram was sent.

7. Men first rode in a balloon on October 15 1783.

8. On April 2 1877 the first human cannonball was fired.

9. July 20 1969 was the day men first landed on the moon.

10. The first adhesive postage stamp appeared on May 1 1840.

Use a comma between the name of a city or town and the name of a state or country.

> The world's oldest zoo is in Vienna, Austria.

What should you do if the two names do not come at the end of a sentence? Put another comma after the name of the state or country.

> Vienna, Austria, is the home of the world's oldest zoo.

Practice 2

Rewrite these sentences on a separate sheet of paper. Use commas wherever they are needed. The first one has been done for you.

1. The first Ferris wheel opened in Chicago Illinois.

   The first Ferris wheel opened in Chicago, Ilinois.

2. A man in Santa Clara California has 1,159 credit cards.

3. The first gas station opened in Bordeaux France.

4. In Enterprise Alabama stands a statue of a boll weevil.

5. A female boxer beat a male opponent in Mexico City Mexico.

6. Basketball was invented in Springfield Massachusetts.

7. The All-American Soap Box Derby is in Akron Ohio.

8. The Gateway Arch is located in St. Louis Missouri.

9. The Dodgers were once a Brooklyn New York team.

10. In Moscow U.S.S.R. a circus has cows that play football.

Lesson 6: Using Commas or Exclamation Points with Interjections

An **interjection** is a word or group of words that expresses feeling. Use a comma after an interjection at the beginning of a sentence.

Oh, I'm not really sure.

Use an exclamation point after an interjection that expresses excitement. Words often used as other parts of speech may become interjections when they express strong feeling.

That really surprises me.

Really! That surprises me.

Practice 1

Rewrite these sentences on a separate sheet of paper. Punctuate each interjection by using either a comma or an exclamation point. The first one has been done for you.

1. Oh Grandma, what big eyes you have!

   Oh! Grandma, what big eyes you have!

2. Ouch I can't believe I ate the whole thing.

3. Yuck Sally just put peanut butter on her eggs.

4. Ah I love the taste of chocolate first thing in the morning.

5. Gosh Toto I don't think we're in Kansas anymore.

6. Wow That's incredible!

7. Well tell us about your exercise program, Mr. T.

8. Hey have you met Rosemary's baby?

9. Darn My toe is caught in the bathtub faucet.

10. Hurrah I'm finished.

Practice 2

Complete the following sentences on a separate sheet of paper by using interjections from the box. Remember to use the correct punctuation marks.

Hey	Well	Wow	Gee	Oh

1. _____ I wouldn't say that.

2. _____ guess who's coming to dinner.

3. _____ why was he asked to help?

4. _____ why can't we talk like everyone else?

5. _____ That's hardly enough time!

Lesson 7: Using Colons, Semicolons, and Hyphens

Use a **colon** to introduce a list of items.

> The photographer brought the following items: cameras, rolls of film, and a tripod.

Use a colon between the hour and the minutes when you use numerals to write expressions of time.

6:15 P.M.   3:00 A.M   11:30 P.M.

Use a colon after the greeting in a business letter.

Dear Mr. Long: Dear Mayor Tyler: Dear Madame:

Practice 1

Rewrite these sentences on a separate sheet of paper. Use a colon wherever it is needed. The first one has been done for you.

1. Yesterday the sun rose at 730 A.M.

   Yesterday the sun rose at 7:30 A.M.

2. The movie doesn't start until 915 P.M.

3. They left the house at 600 A.M.

4. After snowing for two days, the storm finally ended at about 220 P.M.

5. Tim and Roger enjoy the following sports baseball, basketball, and football.

6. The band was made up of the following instruments trumpets, saxophones, trombones, and tubas.

7. Ellen told us about her favorite artists Rembrandt, Renoir, Manet, and Monet.

8. The newspaper is delivered every day at 630 A.M.

9. Larry will visit the following cities Boston, Philadelphia, New York, and Moose Jaw.

10. At 256 A.M. a man set foot on the moon.

You have learned to use a comma when you want to show a pause in a sentence.

> Arnold's hands were cold, so he put on his gloves.

But how would you show a break in thought that is stronger than the pause? You would use a **semicolon**.

> Arnold's hands were cold; he put on his gloves.

Of course, you could just use a period and split the sentence into two separate sentences. But that would show a complete break in thought.

> Arnold's hands were cold. He put on his gloves.

Here's another way to go about using a semicolon. Suppose you have two closely related sentences, such as the ones above. You can join them into one sentence by using a semicolon.

> Arnold's hands were cold. He put on his gloves.

> Arnold's hands were cold; he put on his gloves.

So a semicolon can be used to show an important break in thought in a long sentence. Or it can be used to join two separate sentences into one longer sentence.

Practice 2

Rewrite these sentences on a separate sheet of paper. In each sentence, use a semicolon instead of the comma and the word following the comma. The first one is done for you.

1. Randy got into his car, and he headed toward Lisa's house.

   Randy got into his car; he headed toward Lisa's house.

2. Randy and Lisa had some free time, and they wanted to go to a movie.

3. They turned to the movie section in the newspaper, and they looked through the listings.

4. They could go see an adventure, or they could go see a comedy.

5. Randy liked suspense movies, so he suggested the latest James Bond movie.

6. Lisa liked suspense movies, and she also enjoyed comedies.

7. There was a Richard Pryor movie downtown, and there was a Steve Martin movie in the neighborhood.

8. Randy has just seen the Steve Martin movie, so they decided against that.

9. Time was running out, so they had to decide soon.

10. They decided not to go anywhere, because it was too cold outside.

Challenge

Read the following sentences. Notice how they are related. Combine the two sentences into one sentence by using a semicolon. Write the sentence on a separate sheet of paper

Randy and Lisa turned on the television.
They watched a suspense movie and a comedy.

Use a **hyphen** in compound numbers from twenty-one through ninety-nine.

twenty-two   fifty-three   eighty-seven

Use a hyphen in a fraction.

one-fifth   two-sevenths   one-half

Use hyphens in certain compound words.

great-aunt   commander-in-chief

Practice 3

In the sentences below, find the numbers and fractions that should have hypens. Write them correctly on a separate sheet of paper. The first one is done for you.

1. A couple rode a Ferris wheel for thirty seven days.

   thirty-seven

2. A giant squid's eye can be one and one fourth feet wide.

3. Steak is seventy four percent water.

4. The baby weighed seven and one half pounds.

5. A boy created a house of cards sixty eight stories tall.

6. Reggie Jackson's bat weighs two and one quarter pounds.

7. A hockey puck weighs about one third pound.

8. A man's brain weighs three and one tenth pounds.

9. The comic strip "Blondie" is printed in fifty five nations.

10. An ostrich egg can weigh thirty one pounds.

Challenge

Think about the people in your family, your distant relatives as well as your immediate family. Would you need to use a hyphen to describe any of them in writing? On a separate sheet of paper, write a sentence about one of these family members.

Chapter Review

Chapter Summary

☐ A colon is used to introduce a series of items.

Waving in the breeze were the flags of the following countries: Brazil, Mexico, and Peru.

☐ A comma indicates a short pause between words or groups of words.

If you are going out tonight, don't forget to wear a warm coat.

☐ A hyphen is used between parts of compound numbers, fractions, and certain compound words.

thirty-nine   three-tenths   son-in-law

☐ An interjection is a word that expresses emotion. It is followed by an exclamation point or a comma.

Wow! It's raining cats and dogs!

Oh, I think she is going shopping today.

☐ Quotation marks are used to show the beginning and end of someone's exact words.

Jim said, "We must invite Harry to the party."

☐ A semicolon is used to show a stronger break in thought than that shown by a comma but less than that shown by a period.

They ran inside; it had started to rain.

Chapter Quiz

A. Complete each sentence below. Use the correct word or group of words from the box. Rewrite the sentences on a separate sheet of paper.

colon	comma	hyphen
interjection	quotation marks	semicolon

1. A _____ is used between parts of compound numbers.

2. A _____ indicates a short pause between words.

3. An _____ is a word that expresses emotion.

4. A _____ shows a strong break in thought.

5. _____ show the beginning and end of someone's exact words.

6. A _____ introduces a series of items.

B. Rewrite these sentences on a separate sheet of paper. Use commas wherever they are needed.

1. Albert sat down at his desk opened the book and began to read.

2. Ruth bought apples oranges and bananas at the store.

3. Sally had to take a train two busses and a taxi to get home.

C. Rewrite these sentences on a separate sheet of paper. Use a comma or exclamation point with each interjection. Don't forget to use end punctuation with each sentence.

1. Well you know how I feel about chocolate

2. Wow I think you better report this to the captain

3. Gee what if it rains on Sunday

Unit Review

A. Copy each of these sentences on a separate sheet of paper. Draw one line under the subject of each sentence. Draw two lines under each predicate.

1. Mrs. O'Leary's cow supposedly started the Chicago Fire.

2. Sherlock Holmes lived at 221B Baker Street.

3. Where did Professor Moriarity live?

B. Rewrite this paragraph on a separate sheet of paper. Use capital letters and end punctuation.

have you ever heard the story of jonah he was supposedly swallowed by a whale an english sailor had the same experience in 1891 his whaling boat captured a whale the whale overturned the boat the sailor was swallowed whole by the whale his shipmates killed the whale then they saw its stomach move they cut open the stomach there was the missing sailor what a surprise the sailor was alive

C. Rewrite these sentences on a separate sheet of paper. Use commas with any direct quotations you find.

1. "The bigger they are" a boxer said "the harder they fall."

2. Another boxer said "I zigged when I should have zagged."

3. "When the going gets tough" Rockne said "the tough get going."

Unit Two

Nouns

Chapter 3

Common and Proper Nouns

Look at the photograph. Name some of the persons, places, and things you see. The words you use to name persons, places, and things are nouns.

Chapter Learning Objectives

Identify common and proper nouns.

Use capital letters with proper nouns.

Identify abbreviations.

Use nouns in speaking and writing.

Words to Know

abbreviation   a shortened form of a word

common noun   a word that names any person, place, thing, event, or idea

noun   a word that names a person, place, thing, event, or idea

proper noun   a word that names a particular person, place, thing, event, or idea

Lesson 1: What Are Nouns?

All people and things have names. All people and most things have more than one name. **You** have more than one name. You have the name your parents gave you. You are a **student**. You are a **son** or **daughter**. You are a young **woman** or **man**.

Nouns are nothing new to you. You already know more nouns than are in this whole book. For example, just name the things you ate for dinner last night.

Each word in dark type above could be a name for you. Each word is a **noun**.

Nouns are naming words. A noun may name a person, place, or thing. A noun may name an event. A noun may name an idea. An idea may be a quality or a feeling.

> Persons: man, nurse, sister, people, Jill
>
> Places: street, river, school, Texas
>
> Things: chair, paper, hat
>
> Events: party, rally, concert
>
> Qualities: courage, loyalty
>
> Feelings: love, fear, happiness

To get started, look around the room. Name the things and people you see. You will use nouns to name them.

Thinking Skill: Grouping Nouns

Make five columns on a separate sheet of paper. Use these headings.

Persons	Places	Things	Events	Feelings
student				

List each noun below under the correct heading. The first one is done for you.

student	rock	sadness	concert	store
house	party	courage	teacher	prize
meeting	radio	nurse	cave	fear
joy	field	trial	window	aunt

Challenge

Add one noun of your own under each heading.

Practice 1

Write the nouns from these sentences on a separate sheet of paper. There may be more than one noun in a sentence. The first sentence is done for you.

1. A porcupine can float in water.

   porcupine water

2. Frogs pull in their eyeballs to close their eyes.

3. Penguins are not fish, but they can swim.

4. Was the dodo a smart bird?

5. Doves are actually fierce birds.

6. These divers found no treasure.

7. The furniture in her apartment belongs to her sister.

8. Read the directions on the page.

9. Where are the toothpaste and soap?

10. They are in the suitcase on the bench.

Practice 2

Complete these sentences on a separate sheet of paper. Use nouns of your own. The first sentence is done for you.

1. Nora wants the green _____ .

   Nora wants the green dress.

2. A _____ suddenly rushed in.

3. He took one look at the _____ and laughed.

4. Laurie broke the _____ last _____ .

5. Tim won a _____ at the _____ .

A noun may be a group of words.

A group of words may name a person, place, thing, event, or idea. Some groups have hyphens between the words. Nouns that are a group of words make sense as a group. For example: The noun **ice cream** means something different than the separate nouns **ice** and **cream**.

Can you think of other groups of words that are nouns? How about things that can be found in a home? Example: alarm clock

Read these groups of words. Each one is a noun.

| high school | Fort Mason | commander-in-chief |
| maid-of-honor | Stone Avenue | Mount Baldy |

Practice 3

Write the nouns from these sentences on a separate sheet of paper. Then underline the nouns that are groups of words. The first sentence is done for you.

1. The White House is the home of the president.

   White House home president

2. Jones Beach State Park is near New York City.

3. The man planted forget-me-nots in his garden.

4. The junior high school is next to the high school.

5. Who is vice president of the club?

6. The maid-of-honor was late for the wedding.

7. Is the store on Selby Avenue or Hilltop Drive?

8. People on diets eat ice milk instead of ice cream.

9. How many Nobel Prizes are given each year?

10. Mount McKinley is the highest mountain in North America.

Practice 4

There are 19 nouns in the paragraph below. Write these nouns on a separate sheet of paper. For example, the nouns in the first sentence are **shock** and **morning**.

What a **shock** I had this **morning**! I arrived at school just before the bell rang. I rushed to my locker to get my notebook. I expected to see a messy pile of shoes, sweatshirts, and books. Instead, most of my belongings were neatly piled on the floor. My clothes were hung on hooks. On the shelf was a box wrapped in silver paper. Who had straightened out my locker? What was in the box?

Words to the Wise

Too many cooks spoil the broth.

Write this proverb on a separate sheet of paper. Draw a line under each noun. Then think about what the proverb means. Remember that proverbs always state a truth or give advice. What is the truth behind this statement? Does it just say something about **cooks**—or about everybody? Is it only about **soup**—or about other things as well? Explain the meaning of this wise old saying in your own words.

Lesson 2: Common and Proper Nouns

A **common noun** is the name of any person, place, thing, event, or idea.

A **proper noun** is the name of a particular person, place, thing, event, or idea. Every important word in a proper noun is capitalized.

Name the people in your family. Those names are proper nouns. Then tell how they are related to you. Those words are common nouns.

Persons

Common nouns:	man	athlete	aunt
Proper nouns:	John Tyler	Lou Gehrig	Aunt Anne

Places

Common nouns:	state	country	lake
Proper nouns:	Nevada	France	Lake Mead

Things

Common nouns:	day	month	language
Proper nouns:	Monday	June	English

Practice 1

Find the proper nouns in these sentences. List the proper nouns on a separate sheet of paper. The first sentence is done for you.

1. Cobras kill many people in India every year.

   India

2. Queen Elizabeth of England once visited a tortoise.

3. A snake in the Philadelphia Zoological Gardens bit itself to death.

4. Some New Yorkers believe that alligators live in the sewers.

5. Tarzan learned to swing through the trees.

Practice 2

Rewrite these sentences on a separate sheet of paper. Capitalize the proper nouns. The first sentence is done for you.

1. My sister helen wanted to be a teacher.

   My sister Helen wanted to be a teacher.

2. The hotel biltmore was filled with americans.

3. His friend paul speaks french.

4. Let's go to the concert in central park.

5. I think bugs bunny is a funny rabbit.

6. Last january, debra visited new mexico.

7. People in germany speak german.

Lesson 3: Using Proper Nouns Correctly

List the proper nouns for the place where you live. Start with your street, then your town, and go on from there.

The names of places are proper nouns. Capitalize the important words in the names of places. Short words, such as **of** and **and** are usually not important words.

Streets or Routes:	Oak Street	Route 6
Cities:	Newark	New York City
States:	Maine	North Dakota
Buildings:	Museum of Art	War Memorial
Natural Features:	Mount Shasta	Pacific Ocean

The names of organizations are proper nouns. Capitalize the important words in the names of schools and organizations.

Elm High School   Music Club   American Legion

Practice 1

Rewrite these sentences on a separate sheet of paper. Capitalize the proper nouns. The first sentence is done for you.

1. The south high school history club visited washington, d.c.

   The South High School History Club visited Washington, D.C.

2. They saw the lincoln memorial and the washington monument.

3. They had to wait at the white house.

4. Everyone enjoyed the picnic in rock creek park.

5. They went for a boat ride on the potomac river.

6. Some of the group visited the national gallery of art.

7. They left from national airport on sunday.

Practice 2

Rewrite these addresses correctly on a separate sheet of paper. Use capital letters where necessary.

1. Ms. francie jones
   32 denver place
   los angeles, CA 90067

2. Mr. carl rath
   49 vista drive
   fleming, KY 41816

Sometimes it can be hard to decide if a noun is common or proper. Ask yourself if this word means a region. If so, it is a part of the country and should be capitalized as a proper noun.

Names of parts of the country are proper nouns. Capitalize the names of parts of the country.

In the summer it is hot in the **Southeast.**

Names of directions are common nouns. Do not capitalize names of directions.

We will drive **north** to the White Mountains.

Practice 3

Rewrite these sentences on a separate sheet of paper. Capitalize only the proper nouns. The first sentence is done for you.

1. We want to go from the northeast to the southeast.

   We want to go from the Northeast to the Southeast.

2. We shall drive south until we get to atlanta.

3. How do you get from the northwest to the northeast?

4. You go east.

5. My uncle jed visited the southwest.

6. Is the city of miami in the southeast?

7. The rocky mountains are west of the mississippi river.

8. The cape cod national seashore is in the northeast.

9. To get from utah to the pacific ocean, you go west.

10. The state of vermont is in the northeast.

Name two of your favorite movies. What are the proper nouns in the titles?

Books, movies, magazines, and television programs have titles. Many other things do, too. Titles contain proper nouns. Capitalize each important word in a title. Always capitalize the first and last words in a title.

Children of Dune   "A Rose for Emily"

War and Peace   *The Return of the Native*

Practice 4

Write the titles on a separate sheet of paper. Capitalize all important words. Capitalize the first and last words. The first one is done for you.

1. citizen kane

   Citizen Kane

2. "dover beach"

3. *pride and prejudice*

4. *a tale of two cities*

5. *our town*

6. the gold rush

7. star wars

8. conan the barbarian

9. "the bear"

10. *main street*

Some proper nouns may be shortened. This shortened form is called an **abbreviation**. Capitalize the abbreviations of proper nouns. Put a period at the end of abbreviations.

| Hill Street | Hill **St.** | Doctor Wu | **Dr.** Wu |
| Moore Drive | Moore **Dr.** | Mister Ross | **Mr.** Ross |

Practice 5

There are 25 words in this paragraph that should be capitalized. Rewrite the paragraph on a separate sheet of paper. Use capital letters wherever necessary.

Many famous men got their start in football. Presidents eisenhower, nixon, and ford played football in college. However, mr. nixon did not play much at whittier college in california. President ford played center at the university of michigan. He even got offers from the chicago bears and the detroit lions. A man named "Whizzer" white did play for the detroit lions. Later, justice byron white became a member of the supreme court of the united states.

Challenge

Think about the names of people you know and the streets you travel on. Write these names on a separate sheet of paper. Use abbreviations wherever possible.

Chapter Review

Chapter Summary

☐ A noun names a person, place, thing, event, or idea.

Noun: cat

☐ A common noun is the name of any person, place, thing, event or idea.

Common noun: woman

☐ A proper noun is the name of a particular person, place, thing, event, or idea.

Proper noun: Clara Barton

☐ A noun may be a group of words. Sometimes there are hyphens between these words.

Nouns that are groups of words: ice cream maid-of-honor

☐ An abbreviation is the shortened form of a word.

Abbreviation: Mr. Jones

Chapter Quiz

A. Complete each sentence with the correct word from the box. Write the sentences on a separate sheet of paper.

abbreviation	noun	common	proper

1. A _____ is a naming word.

2. A _____ noun can be the special name of a particular person.

3. An _____ is a shortened form of a word.

4. A _____ noun can be the general name of a type of thing.

B. Write each noun from the sentences on a separate sheet of paper. If it is a common noun, write **C** after it. If it is a proper noun, write **P**.

1. The oldest subway is in London.

2. Long ago on April Fool's Day, the first car was sold.

3. If Michael comes, he will bring a cake.

4. Do you prefer Roger Rabbit or Bugs Bunny?

C. Rewrite these sentences on a separate sheet of paper. Capitalize the proper nouns.

1. In which part of the united states is the state of oregon?

2. Oregon is north of california, and the pacific ocean forms its western border.

3. The city of salem is the capital of oregon, but portland is the largest city.

4. A man called Ken Kesey wrote a book called *sometimes a great notion.*

Chapter 4 Other Nouns

Imagine that you are going shopping in the supermarket in this photograph. Notice that there are more than one of each of the items for sale. Describe what is on the shelves. You will have to use plural nouns.

Chapter Learning Objectives

Use singular and plural nouns.

Spell plural nouns.

Form possessive nouns.

Use concrete and abstract nouns.

Use specific nouns.

Words to Know

abstract noun   a noun that names an idea or quality

apostrophe ’   a punctuation mark that is used to show that something belongs to a person or thing

concrete noun   a noun that names something that can be seen, heard, touched, smelled, or tasted

plural noun   a noun that names more than one person, place, thing, event, or idea

possessive noun   a noun that shows ownership or relationship

singular noun   a noun that names one person, place, thing, event, or idea

specific noun   a noun that gives more information about a person, place, or thing

Lesson 1: Singular and Plural Nouns

A **singular noun** names one person, place, thing, event, or idea.

A **plural noun** names more than one person, place, thing, event, or idea.

Singular Nouns	Plural Nouns
book	books
house	houses
bush	bushes

Practice 1

On a separate sheet of paper, write each of the nouns listed below. If the noun is singular, write **S**. If the noun is plural, write **P**. The first one is done for you.

1. worker **S**
2. games
3. thought
4. campground
5. dancers

6. hopes
7. fair
8. tickets
9. streets
10. clock

Thinking Skill: Grouping Singular and Plural Nouns

Make two columns on a separate sheet of paper. Use these headings.

Singular Nouns	Plural Nouns

List each noun below under the correct heading.

pencil
letter
singers
woman
record
concerts

garden
libraries
song
men
job
hopes

writers
legs
speeches
cameras
friendship
dancer

Add two more nouns of your own to each column.

Practice 2

List the nouns in each of these sentences on a separate sheet of paper. If a noun is singular, write **S** after it. If a noun is plural, write **P** after it. The first sentence is done for you.

1. Let's make plans for our trip next year.

   plans P, trip S, year S

2. The story is about a scientist and a frightened ghost.

3. All my cousins were at the picnic.

4. Ivan enjoys the peace and quiet of the mountains.

5. Several floats and marching bands were in the parade.

6. We set up our tents near a stream.

7. These hills are covered with wildflowers for months.

8. Clouds hid the sun, and rain fell on the field.

9. The manager asks for ideas and suggestions from the employees.

10. She thought about the dance and her friends.

Lesson 2: Spelling Plural Nouns Correctly

The plural of most nouns is made by adding **s**. But nouns that end with **-x, -s, -z, -ch,** or **-sh** are treated differently. Make the plural of these nouns by adding **es**.

Singular Nouns	Plural Nouns
box	boxes
guess	guesses
lunch	lunches
flash	flashes
buzz	buzzes

Practice 1

On a separate sheet of paper, write the plural of each noun. The first one is done for you.

1. tax **taxes**	5. business	9. watch
2. wish	6. dress	10. beach
3. wax	7. leash	11. waltz
4. sandwich	8. clash	12. dish

Some nouns end with **-ay, -ey,** or **-oy**. Make the plural of these nouns by adding **s**.

Singular Nouns	Plural Nouns
day	days
turkey	turkeys
joy	joys

Some nouns end with a consonant and **-y**. Make the plural of these nouns by changing the **y** to **i** and adding **es**.

Syzygy is a strange word. Most people have never heard of it. But you can find it in a dictionary. How do you think the plural is spelled?

pony   ponies

candy   candies

duty   duties

Practice 2

Rewrite these sentences on a separate sheet of paper. Make each noun plural. The first one is done for you.

1. Where did you put my key?

     Where did you put my keys?

2. Take the toy to the baby.

3. The best race will be the relay.

4. They rode the donkey into the valley.

5. The fly landed on the strawberry.

6. The stairway led down to the bay.

7. Let's go to the library after class.

8. The bright ray lit up the sky.

9. Susan wrote the essay on the weekend.

10. Don had to walk through the alley to get to the dock.

Some nouns end with **-f** or **-ff.**

Make the plural of some of these nouns by adding **s.**

Make the plural of others in two steps: 1) Change the **f** to **v.** 2) Add **es.**

Singular Nouns	Plural Nouns
chef	chefs
cliff	cliffs
gulf	gulfs
leaf	leaves
half	halves
scarf	scarves

Practice 3

A parenthesis is used to set off a word or group of words from the rest of the sentence.

Rewrite these sentences on a separate sheet of paper. Make the noun in the parenthesis plural. This is a parenthesis ( ). The first one is done for you.

1. The boat came too near the (reef).

    The boat came too near the reefs.

2. The men introduced their (wife).

3. Please cut the (loaf) of fresh bread.

4. The detective found both (half) of the letter.

5. Stop (thief)!

6. The (cliff) overlook the ocean.

7. The (chef) wore red (scarf) around their necks.

8. The autumn (leaf) were beautiful this year.

Some nouns end with **-o** or **-oo**. Make the plural of these nouns by adding **s**.

Singular Nouns	Plural Nouns
radio	radios
trio	trios
zoo	zoos
kangaroo	kangaroos

Some nouns end with a consonant and **-o**. Make the plural of these nouns by adding **es**.

Singular Nouns	Plural Nouns
hero	heroes
tomato	tomatoes
potato	potatoes

Some nouns that end with a consonant and **-o** tell about music. Make these nouns plural by adding **s**.

Singular Nouns	Plural Nouns
piano	pianos
soprano	sopranos
contralto	contraltos

Some nouns become plural by changing inside letters.

Singular Nouns	Plural Nouns
woman	women
man	men
foot	feet
mouse	mice
tooth	teeth

Some nouns are the same in the singular and the plural.

Singular Nouns	Plural Nouns
fish	fish
deer	deer
sheep	sheep
series	series

Practice 4

Rewrite these sentences on a separate sheet of paper. Make the noun in the parenthesis plural. The first one is done for you.

1. Tomorrow I shall have my (tooth) cleaned.
   Tomorrow I shall have my teeth cleaned.

2. Two (piano) accompanied the (soprano).

3. Several (radio) were playing loudly.

4. Tom and Eduardo are (hero).

5. There are three (series) of questions on the test.

6. We ate five (fish) for dinner.

7. I made a dish with (tomato) and (potato).

8. Both (deer) and (sheep) have four (foot).

9. In this country (kangaroo) can only be seen in (zoo).

10. Ten (man) and twelve (woman) listened to the (trio).

11. Myra broke two (dish).

Practice 5

Seventeen plural nouns are misspelled in the sentences below. On a separate sheet of paper, spell those nouns correctly. Not every plural noun is misspelled. The first sentence has been done for you.

1. Many citys have excellent librarys.

    cities libraries

2. The chefs baked twenty loafs of bread.

3. The boxs were filled with sandwichs, tomatos, and fruit.

4. Two heros caught the thiefs who stole the radioes.

5. Those mans are complaining of sore foots.

6. One of his duties is feeding the ponys and sheeps.

7. Lin caught seventeen fishes.

8. You will find the dishs in the cupboard.

9. The cat caught two more mouses.

10. The dentist has to work on three of my tooths.

Words
to the Wise

Two wrongs can never make a right.

Write this proverb on a separate sheet of paper. Draw a line under the plural noun. Remember that a proverb is a folk saying that states a truth or gives advice. Explain what this proverb means in your own words. Hint: The **wrong** in this proverb means an evil or unjust act.

Lesson 3: Possessive Nouns

The apostrophe is a handy little invention. Imagine how complicated things would be without it. Instead of saying "the Baxters' cat," for example, you would have to say "the cat that belongs to the Baxters."

A **possessive noun** shows ownership or relationship.

Ownership	Relationship
Robert's voice	Theo's uncle
my aunt's house	Ms. Todd's husband
the Baxters' cat	the boys' cousin

Make most singular nouns possessive by adding an **apostrophe ʼ** and an **s**.

When a singular noun ends with **-s**, you may add an apostrophe and an **s** or just an apostrophe.

Make most plural nouns possessive by adding an apostrophe.

Some plural nouns do not end with **-s**. Make these plural nouns possessive by adding an apostrophe and an **s**.

women's   men's   oxen's   deer's

Practice 1

Read these sentences. Write only the possessive nouns on a separate sheet of paper. The first one is done for you.

1. We have tickets for tomorrow night's concert.

   night's

2. Those stories' plots are exciting.

3. All my aunts and uncles will be at my cousin's house.

4. The team's players read the season's schedule.

5. These jeans' prices are too high.

6. That TV series' stars won several awards.

7. Why don't you ask Ted's sister to the club's party.

8. The coach's suggestions increased the players' scores.

9. The evening's entertainment finished with a short skit.

10. Everyone liked the carpenter's work.

11. Two girls' laughter could be heard across the room.

12. Who designed the magazine's cover?

13. Margarita's parents visited her sisters.

Practice 2

Rewrite these sentences on a separate sheet of paper. Make the noun in the parenthesis possessive. The first one is done for you.

1. Next week is (Secretaries) Week.

   Next week is Secretaries' Week.

2. This (lesson) subject is possessive nouns.

3. (Reggie) brothers like to play chess.

4. Keep the (boxes) contents a secret.

5. Mrs. Rudolph answered the (women) questions.

6. The two (parties) candidates debated the issues.

7. The (candidates) ideas seemed far apart.

8. (Waldo) grandmother is visiting him.

9. He will replace his (watch) broken strap.

10. That (library) large collection is very useful.

Practice 3

Rewrite these sentences on a separate sheet of paper. Put a possessive noun of your own in each sentence. The first one is done for you.

1. The _____ water supply is getting low.

   The town's water supply is getting low.

2. What is your _____ name.
3. The exercises left the _____ legs sore.
4. The _____ dessert was fruit.
5. Randy met the _____ father.
6. The _____ crops are blackberries and potatoes.

Thinking Skill: Grouping Possessive and Plural Nouns

Make two columns on a separate sheet of paper. Use these headings.

Possessive Nouns	Plural Nouns

List each noun below under the correct heading.

newspaper's	uncles	painters'
towns	women's	heads

Challenge

Add a noun of your own under each heading.

Lesson 4: Concrete and Abstract Nouns

A **concrete noun** names something you can see, hear, touch, smell, or taste.

An **abstract noun** names an idea or a quality.

Abstract Nouns	Concrete Nouns
strength	elephant
beauty	flower
patriotism	flag

Practice 1

On a separate sheet of paper, write the abstract noun from each group. The first group has been done for you.

1. chicken   apple   hunger   ice cream

   hunger

2. bicycle   car   airplane   transportation
3. smile   happiness   laugh   joke
4. weather   storm   sunshine   rain
5. kitten   baby   flower   weakness
6. fire   smoke   danger   flames
7. house   shelter   apartment   hut

Practice 2

Complete these sentences with an abstract noun from the box. Write the sentences on a separate sheet of paper. The first one is done for you.

Each word in the box is an abstract noun because it names a quality.

pleasure	humor	fault	selfishness	hunger
greed	courage	joy	peace	sorrow

1. A person with a good sense of _____ makes me laugh.

   A person with a good sense of humor makes me laugh.

2. Dean's stomach was growling with _____ .

3. It takes _____ to face trouble head on.

4. The treaty signed after the war brought _____ .

5. Barry's greatest _____ is his laziness.

6. They cried in _____ over the loss of their pet.

7. In our _____ , we took every last one.

8. The fans showed their _____ by cheering.

9. In her happiness, Martha jumped for _____ .

10. Benton, who never helps others, suffers from _____ .

Thinking Skill: Giving Examples

Number a separate sheet of paper from 1 to 5. Read each sentence in column A. The words in dark type are abstract nouns. Copy these nouns. Then find the sentence in column B that shows the meaning of each abstract noun. Write the correct meaning next to each number. For example, next to number 1, write **He gave many presents.**

A	B
1. Nick's **generosity** was known to all his friends.	He wrote a thank-you note to anyone who did anything for him.
2. His brother's **selfishness** was just as well known.	He gave many presents.
3. Many of her actions showed **courage**.	Any sudden noise made it hide.
4. Manny never failed to show his **gratitude**.	Although he had plenty of time, he never helped anyone.
5. The dog often showed **fear**.	She dove into icy water to rescue a drowning child.

Challenge

Write three abstract nouns of your own.

Lesson 5: Specific Nouns

A **specific noun** gives more information about a person, place, or thing than a nonspecific noun.

Nonspecific Nouns	Specific Nouns
animal	lion
flower	tulip
insect	bee

Practice 1

Food is a noun. It is an important part of your daily life. But it is not a specific noun. Why not?

The nouns in the box are specific. The nouns in dark type in the sentences below are nonspecific. Rewrite the sentences on a separate sheet of paper. Change each nonspecific noun to a specific noun. You may use the nouns in the box. For example, in the first sentence, write **diamond** instead of **stone**.

roses	bird	doctor	pianist	dog
diamond	howl	gardener	ham	apples

1. In the center of the ring was a large **stone**.
2. The **creature** was building a nest.
3. The dog let out a **terrible noise**.
4. That **person** sees many patients.
5. Jesse bought some **fruit**.
6. Do you want some **meat** with your eggs?
7. Please cut some **flowers** for the table.
8. Some **animal** dug a hole in the yard.
9. The **woman** played well.
10. That **man** takes good care of our garden.

Challenge

Choose one of the sentences in Practice 1. Replace the specific noun there with one of your own. Write the new sentence on your paper.

Thinking Skill: Giving Examples

Copy the chart on a separate sheet of paper.

Nonspecific Nouns	Specific Nouns
person	athlete
machine	
store	
people	
bug	

The nouns in this list are nonspecific. In the second column, write a specific noun for each noun listed. The first one is done for you.

Chapter Review

Chapter Summary

☐ A singular noun names one person, place, thing, event, or idea.

Singular noun: student

☐ A plural noun names more than one person, place, thing, event, or idea.

Plural noun: students

☐ A possessive noun shows ownership or relationship. An aspostrophe is used with possessive nouns.

Possessive nouns: student's students'

☐ A concrete noun names something you can see, hear, touch, taste, or smell.

Concrete noun: apple

☐ An abstract noun names a quality or an idea.

Abstract noun: sweetness

☐ A specific noun tells more than a noun that is nonspecific.

Specific noun: pear

Nonspecific noun: fruit

Chapter Quiz

Complete each sentence with a word from the box. Write the sentences on a separate sheet of paper.

singular	abstract	plural
concrete	possessive	specific

1. The noun **singer** is more _____ than the noun **person**.

2. Make the _____ form of most plural nouns by adding an apostrophe.

3. A noun that names something you can hear, see, touch, taste, or smell is a _____ noun.

4. A _____ noun names one person, place, thing, event, or idea.

5. A noun that names an idea or quality is an _____ noun.

6. A _____ noun names more than one person, place, thing, event, or idea.

B. Write the nouns from these sentences on a separate sheet of paper. Write **S** if the noun is singular. Write **P** if the noun is plural. Then, if the noun is possessive, write **Pos** after the **P** or **S**.

1. Katie's talent for tuning pianos is amazing.

2. Those fish with the blue stripes used to be Cliff's.

3. After five day's work, the women took two days off.

C. Rewrite these sentences on a separate sheet of paper. Choose the specific noun in each sentence.

1. (Animals, lions) live on the plains in Africa.

2. That woman is a (worker, lawyer).

3. His idea of fun is playing (chess, games).

Unit Review

A. There are 17 nouns in these sentences. Write them on a separate sheet of paper.

1. Ali just came to our high school.

2. The Hendersons' new house is in Kankakee.

3. The dog's leg is broken.

4. Fear stopped them in their tracks.

5. We had ice cream after dinner.

6. An elm is a tree.

7. The Smiths drove north to Vermont.

8. I read *The Little Prince* to the children.

B. Make each noun plural. Write the nouns on a separate sheet of paper.

  1. table   2. fox   3. deer   4. woman   5. monkey

C. Make each noun possessive. Write the nouns on a separate sheet of paper.

  1. friend 2. students 3. men 4. Gerry 5. group

Unit Three

Pronouns

Chapter 5   Pronouns and Antecedents

You have learned that nouns are used to name persons, places, things, events, and ideas. In this chapter you will learn about pronouns. Pronouns are used to take the place of nouns or of groups of words that include a noun. All the people and things you see in this photograph can be named by pronouns as well as by nouns.

Chapter Learning Objectives

Use personal pronouns in a sentence.

Identify antecedents.

Use possessive pronouns in a sentence.

Use indefinite pronouns in a sentence.

Words to Know

antecedent the noun or nouns that the pronoun replaces

indefinite pronoun a pronoun that does not replace a particular noun

personal pronoun a word that takes the place of a noun, a group of nouns, or a group of words that includes a noun

possessive pronoun a pronoun that shows ownership or relationship

reflexive pronoun a pronoun that refers back to a noun or pronoun already named

Lesson 1: Personal Pronouns

A **personal pronoun** takes the place of a noun, a group of nouns, or a group of words that includes a noun.

Earnest hit the ball.

> **He** hit **it**.

Bill and Kim watched.

> **They** watched.

The three girls left.

> **They** left.

Where is the big green plate?

> Where is **it**?

Personal Pronouns			
I	it	her	us
he	me	we	they
she	him	you	them

Practice 1

Write the personal pronouns from these sentences on a separate sheet of paper. The first one is done for you.

You have been using personal pronouns ever since you learned how to talk. I and me are the favorite words of most children.

1. We often go camping with him.

    We him

2. She sent me a postcard from New York.

3. Were they completely satisfied with it?

4. I will bake a cake for you.

5. Give them to us later, please.

6. They will help us tomorrow.

7. She thought he would bring it.

8. Where did you put them?

Practice 2

Replace the words in dark type with the correct pronoun. Rewrite the sentences on a separate sheet of paper. The first one is done for you.

1. **Gina** wrapped **the gift** in blue paper.

    She wrapped it in blue paper.

2. **Mr. Krantz** will fix **the sprinkler**.

3. **Rick and Sal** took **the photographs**.

4. Borrow **the tape** from **Babette**.

5. **All the team members** are counting on **John**.

6. **Bruce** is studying **that book** carefully.

7. **Davis** plays **the piano** every day.

8. **Pam and Jessie** told **Will** about **the party**.

9. **The question** puzzled **Judy**.

10. Only **Lou** knew **the answers**.

The word or group of words that a pronoun replaces is called its **antecedent**.

> **Meg** is fond of jigsaw puzzles. **She** bought a new puzzle today.

antecedent: **Meg**   pronoun: **she**

> Mary invited **Brad and Lewis**, but **they** can't come.

antecedent: **Brad and Lewis**   pronoun: **they**

> **Levi the cat** likes people to pet **him**.

antecedent: **Levi the cat**   pronoun: **him**

Practice 3

Copy these sentences on a separate sheet of paper. Find the antecedent for each pronoun. Draw a line under the pronoun. Draw two lines under the antecedent. The first sentence has been done for you.

1. Alex and Tracy asked Sharon to go with them.

   Alex and Tracy asked Sharon to go with them.

2. That book is interesting because it tells a true story.

3. Mrs. Rogers, will you be home tomorrow?

4. Ed was here, but he had to leave.

5. Bob called to Jan, but she did not hear.

6. Cal spoke to Li and Juan when they arrived.

A pronoun must agree with its antecedent. "Agree with" means to be the same in number and person. If the antecedent is singular, the pronoun must be singular.

> Robin will wash the **floor** and wax **it**.

> Take one **onion** and mince **it**.

If the antecedent is plural, the pronoun must be plural.

> When the **berries** are ripe, the boys will pick **them**. **Grace and Ana** know **they** will be late.

Check pronoun-antecedent agreement by saying a sentence out loud. Most often a mistake sounds wrong.

If the antecedent is masculine, the pronoun must be masculine.

> **Mr. Perez** goes fishing whenever **he** can. While **Jim** is speaking, don't interrupt **him**.

If the antecedent is feminine, the pronoun must be feminine.

> **Sandra** asked Tom to help **her**.

> **Gloria** will come if **she** can.

Practice 4

Complete these sentences on a separate sheet of paper with pronouns of your own. Remember that a pronoun must agree with its antecedent. The first one is done for you.

1. John invited Mary to visit _____ next week.

   John invited Mary to visit him next week.

2. When you finished the book, where did you put _____ ?

3. Open the door for Raul when _____ rings the bell.

4. I wanted Paul to play the piano, but _____ played the drums instead.

5. Ruby asked Linda to drive _____ to the station.

Lesson 2: Reflexive Pronouns

A **reflexive pronoun** refers back to a noun or pronoun already named. Reflexive pronouns end in **-self** or **-selves**. The words in the box are reflexive pronouns.

myself	ourselves
yourself	yourselves
herself himself itself	themselves

A reflexive pronoun is used in two ways in a sentence. It adds new information and it gives extra importance to the word it refers to.

Robert washed the dishes **himself**.

Robert **himself** washed the dishes.

Practice 1

Find the reflexive pronouns in these sentences. Write them on a separate sheet of paper. The first one is done for you.

1. Rosalie knitted that sweater herself.

   herself

2. Carlos said that he needed to be by himself.

3. Did you make the decorations yourselves?

4. They seldom do anything for themselves.

5. She herself answered the question.

Practice 2

Complete these sentences by using a reflexive pronoun. Write the sentences on a separate sheet of paper. The first one is done for you.

1. Ken and Angelo prepared the meal _____ .

   Ken and Angelo prepared the meal themselves.

2. Bonnie wanted the bicycle for _____ .

3. The problem may take care of _____ .

4. We have decided to paint the house _____ .

5. You can do that for _____ .

Practice 3

The pronouns in dark type do not agree with their antecedents. Rewrite the sentences with the correct pronouns on another sheet of paper. The first one is done for you.

1. You two should be proud of **yourself.**

    You two should be proud of yourselves.

2. One tree in the woods stood by **themselves.**

3. The brothers planted the garden **himself.**

4. All of us fool **themselves** sometimes.

5. The women took care of it by **herself.**

Lesson 3: Possessive Pronouns

A **possessive pronoun** shows ownership or relationship. Some possessive pronouns come before nouns.

This is Jill's book.   The Smiths' dog is very playful.

This is **her** book.   **Their** dog is very playful.

Possessive Pronouns That Are Used Before Nouns	
my	our
your	your
his her its	their

Practice 1

Find the possessive pronouns. Write them on a separate sheet of paper. The first one is done for you.

1. Here are our cousins from Detroit.

   our

2. I just washed my hair.

3. Their guitars came from Spain.

4. How old is her brother?

5. Your kite is beautiful.

6. Do you prefer my car or his car?

7. That tree lost all its leaves.

8. The artist forgot to sign her name.

Practice 2

Complete these sentences with a possessive pronoun from the box on page 85. Write the sentences on a separate sheet of paper. The first one is done for you.

1. The Gundersons remodeled _____ house last year.

   The Gundersons remodeled their house last year.

2. Penny is training _____ dog.

3. Matt and I will bring _____ skates.

4. Hugh stayed home because of _____ cold.

5. You look just like _____ uncle.

to the Wise

A fool and his money are soon parted.

Write this proverb on a separate sheet of paper. Draw a line under the possessive pronoun. Remember that a proverb is a folk saying that states a truth or gives advice. Explain what this proverb means in your own words.

Some possessive pronouns cannot be used before nouns.

> This book is Margie's.
>
> This book is **hers**.
>
> That car belongs to Kay and Tony.
>
> That car belongs to **them**.

Possessive Pronouns That Are Used Alone in Sentences	
mine	ours
yours	yours
his hers its	theirs

The possessive pronouns his and its can be used alone in a sentence. But they can also be used before a noun.

Practice 3

Find the possessive pronouns in these sentences. Write them on a separate sheet of paper. The first one is done for you.

1. Which apartment is theirs?

   theirs

2. I bought mine at the supermarket.

3. I prefer ours.

4. Is that pen hers?

5. She liked yours and mine best.

6. We have had ours for years.

7. The Marlows will lend us one of theirs.

8. Roy tells me his is missing.

9. I shall bring mine, and you can bring yours.

10. Selena can recognize hers easily.

Practice 4

Rewrite these sentences on a separate sheet of paper. Choose the correct pronoun. The first one is done for you.

1. Which mitts are (your, yours)?

   Which mitts are yours?

2. They say the prize should be (theirs, their).

3. Tell us which seats are (our, ours).

4. She says (her, hers) were burned in the fire.

5. They are always bragging about (their, theirs).

6. How many of (my, mine) are left?

Lesson 4: Indefinite Pronouns

A pronoun that does not take the place of a particular noun is called an **indefinite pronoun**. The antecedent of an indefinite pronoun often is not known.

Everyone heard the noise.

Someone or **something** was in the next room.

All looked.

No one and **nothing** was found.

The words in the boxes are indefinite pronouns.

Singular Indefinite Pronouns		
another	everybody	nothing
anybody	everyone	one
anyone	everything	other
anything	neither	somebody
each	nobody	someone
either	no one	something

Plural Indefinite Pronouns			
both	few	many	several

Indefinite Pronouns That May Be Singular or Plural					
all	any	most	none	some	such

Practice 1

Find the indefinite pronouns in these sentences. Write them on a separate sheet of paper. The first one is done for you.

Anybody *is an indefinite pronoun because it doesn't refer to any particular person. Why do you think* somebody *is an indefinite pronoun?*

1. Does anybody know anything about computers?

   anybody anything

2. Both were invited, but neither came.

3. Some were easy, but most were difficult.

4. All will be judged carefully before any is chosen.

5. Many went to the museum, but few saw everything.

6. Does anyone want another?

7. Nobody had time to do either.

8. Although I tried on several, none fit.

9. If each brings some, there will be many.

10. Everyone waited for someone to say something.

Practice 2

Complete these sentences with an indefinite pronoun. Write these sentences on a separate sheet of paper. The first one is done for you.

1. Here is _____ Charlene would like.

   Here is something Charlene would like.

2. Is _____ there?

3. It looks like _____ was here.

4. Teddi wants to tell _____ about the trip.

5. _____ can come on Thursday.

6. He bought _____ but gave _____ away.

Thinking Skill: Grouping Pronouns

Make three columns on a separate sheet of paper. Use these headings.

Pronouns

Personal	Possessive	Indefinite

List each of these pronouns under the correct heading.

someone	her	theirs	anyone	they
we	nothing	ours	me	nobody
them	mine	neither	I	most

Challenge

Add a pronoun of your own under each heading.

Chapter Review

Chapter Summary

☐ A personal pronoun can take the place of a noun, a group of nouns, or a group of words that includes a noun.

Personal pronoun: you

☐ An antecedent is the noun or nouns that the pronoun replaces. A pronoun must agree with its antecedent.

Antecedent: Rosa

Pronoun: she

Antecedent: Jim and Burt

Pronoun: they

☐ A reflexive pronoun refers back to a noun or pronoun already named.

Reflexive pronoun: herself

☐ A possessive pronoun shows ownership or relationship.

Possessive pronoun: our

☐ An indefinite pronoun does not replace a particular noun. The antecedent often is not known.

Indefinite pronoun: anybody

Chapter Quiz

A. Complete these sentences with a word from the box. Write the sentences on a separate sheet of paper.

indefinite	antecedent	possessive	reflexive

1. A pronoun must agree with its _____ .

2. An _____ pronoun may have an unknown antecedent.

3. Some _____ pronouns can be used before nouns.

4. A _____ pronoun refers back to a noun or pronoun already named.

B. Write the pronouns from these sentences on a separate sheet of paper. If a pronoun is possessive, write **P** after it. If a pronoun is indefinite, write **I** after it. If a pronoun is reflexive, write **R** after it.

1. Margo herself will wallpaper her kitchen.

2. Nothing could stop Max from talking.

3. Is that yours or theirs?

4. Few liked its unusual taste.

5. They will enjoy their visit to his house.

C. Complete these sentences with a possessive pronoun of your own. Write the sentences on a separate sheet of paper.

1. Can a leopard change _____ spots?

2. Why don't bees bend _____ knees?

3. Is that cat wearing _____ hat?

4. Does that puppy fetch _____ pipe and slippers?

5. Is that pet snake really _____ ?

Pronouns That Ask and Point

The pronouns you will study in this chapter help you to form questions and to point out people, places, and things. Some of the pronouns tell more about nouns and other pronouns.

Chapter Learning Objectives

Use interrogative pronouns in a sentence.

Use demonstrative pronouns in a sentence.

Use relative pronouns in a sentence.

Words to Know

demonstrative pronoun a pronoun that points out one or more persons, places, or things

interrogative pronoun a pronoun that is used to ask a question

relative pronoun a pronoun that connects a noun or pronoun with a group of words that tells more about it

Lesson 1: Pronouns That Ask

An **interrogative pronoun** is used to ask a question.

The words in the box are interrogative pronouns.

what	which	who	whom	whose

☐ **Who** and **whom** refer to a person or persons.
Who are those men?
For **whom** is this bouquet?

☐ **Whose** is used when asking about ownership or relationship.
Whose is that?

☐ **What** refers to persons, places, and ideas.
What is in the bag?

☐ **Which** is used when there is a choice between two or more persons, places, or things.
Which do you want?

Practice 1

Find the interrogative pronouns. Some sentences have more than one interrogative pronoun. Write the interrogative pronouns on a separate sheet of paper. The first one is done for you.

1. Whose jacket is it?

   Whose

2. Who is on the phone, and whom are they calling?
3. Which of the three contestants won?
4. What is the meaning of this noise?
5. Whose car was stolen?
6. Who won the Heiseman Trophy last year?
7. What caused the quarrel?
8. For whom is this package, and who sent it?
9. Which seems to you to be the best choice?
10. Who came to the office, and what did he want?

Practice 2

Complete these sentences with interrogative pronouns. Write the sentences on a separate sheet of paper. The first one is done for you.

1. By _____ was that song recorded?

   By whom was that song recorded?

2. _____ handwriting is on the envelope?

3. _____ were the guests?

4. _____ are you doing on Sunday?

5. _____ of the students made this science project?

6. For _____ did you work last summer?

7. To _____ was the letter addressed?

8. _____ of your assignments will you do first?

Practice 3

Write the pronouns from these sentences on a separate sheet of paper. If the pronoun is interrogative, write **I** after it. If the pronoun is indefinite, write **Ind**. If the pronoun is possessive, write **P**. The first one is done for you.

1. Which of the students asked for directions?

   Which I

2. Jerry thinks someone should answer.

3. Has anyone called?

4. Her eyes are blue.

5. Next to whom do you want to sit?

Lesson 2: Demonstrative Pronouns

A **demonstrative pronoun** points out one or more persons, places, or things.

that	these	this	those

That is my favorite place.

These are your letters.

Please give me **those**.

Then he handed me **this**.

Practice 1

Find the demonstrative pronouns. There may be more than one demonstrative pronoun in a sentence. Write the demonstrative pronouns on a separate sheet of paper. The first one is done for you.

1. This is a serious problem.

   This

2. Are those the cookies you baked?

3. That happened only once.

4. I think these used to belong to him.

5. Is this more valuable than that?

6. If only these belong to you, who owns those?

7. That is broken, but this is fine.

8. The jeweler showed me this.

Practice 2

On a separate sheet of paper, write each pronoun. If the pronoun is demonstrative, write **D** after it. If the pronoun is interrogative, write **I**. The first sentence is done for you.

1. Who would do that?

   Who I that D

2. This is Robert's favorite part.

3. Which of these did Sheila buy?

4. Those are the rules.

5. By whom was that written?

6. What could have happened to this?

Words to the Wise

Those who complain most are most to be complained of.

Write this proverb on a separate sheet of paper. Draw a line under the demonstrative pronoun. Remember that a proverb states a truth. Do you agree with this proverb? Think about people you know. Explain what this proverb means in your own words.

Lesson 3: Relative Pronouns

A **relative pronoun** connects a noun or pronoun with a group of words that tells more about it.

The words in the box are relative pronouns.

that	which	who	whom	whose

The way a pronoun is used in a sentence tells you what kind of pronoun it is.

☐ **Who** and **whom** refer to a person or persons.
The woman **who** is speaking is my aunt.
The man **whom** I spoke to is my uncle.

☐ **Whose** shows ownership or relationship.
The man **whose** dog is lost offered a reward for its return.

☐ **That** and **which** refer to places or things.
The pie **that** Nora baked is delicious.
The book, **which** has a red cover, is not on the shelf.

Relative pronouns have antecedents. Relative pronouns refer to a noun or pronoun in the sentence. This noun or pronoun usually comes just before the relative pronoun.

The **house that** Jack built has a strange history.

antecedent: **house**   relative pronoun: **that**

Practice 1

Find the relative pronouns. Write them on a separate sheet of paper. The first one is done for you.

1. She could find no one who spoke English.

   who

2. Ted has a voice that carries far.
3. We preferred the watch that we saw at Jensen's.
4. She was a woman whose ideas were ahead of her time.
5. The couple whom they interviewed saw the accident.
6. The man who spoke first was very funny.
7. Jenny will know a restaurant that has good food.
8. We need someone whom we can trust.
9. Have you seen the man who moved next door?
10. The hammer, which you were looking for, is in the drawer.

Practice 2

Write these sentences on a separate sheet of paper. Put one line under the relative pronoun. Put two lines under the antecedent. The first one is done for you.

1. The dress that she wore had yellow stripes.
   The <u>dress</u> <u>that</u> she wore had yellow stripes.

2. Let's talk to someone who can help us.
3. Is Arturo the uncle whom I met?

4. Frances selected a plant that blooms.

5. Here are my friends whose dog had puppies.

6. That is the actress whom we saw in the play.

7. Look for a house that has white shutters.

8. The plumber whose work we like best is away.

9. The person who bought this gift is thoughtful.

10. The pizza, which nobody wanted, was given to the dog.

Practice 3

Complete these sentences with relative pronouns of your own. Write the sentences on a separate sheet of paper. The first one is done for you.

1. The dog _____ I want is a boxer.

   The dog that I want is a boxer.

2. The woman _____ came to the door did not live there.

3. The records _____ are on the table are his.

4. The girl _____ kitten got lost was very sad.

5. The story _____ he told was unbelievable.

Challenge

Things that are **relative** have something in common. The members of your family are called your **relatives**. Think of two more words in this word family that show connection.

Practice 4

Each sentence contains an interrogative, a demonstrative, or a relative pronoun. Write these pronouns on a separate sheet of paper. Write **I** after an interrogative pronoun. Write **D** after a demonstrative pronoun. Write **R** after a relative pronoun. The first sentence is done for you.

1. That has always been my favorite program.

   That   D

2. Which of these movies would you like to see?

3. I have seen all the movies that I had wanted to see.

4. What do you think he wanted?

5. The person who can answer the question is Samuel.

6. Give me that, please.

7. Irene did not know which her husband had chosen.

8. The ring that Jackie prefers is too expensive.

9. Who will go with us?

10. Send these to Mrs. Alwyn.

Chapter Review

Chapter Summary

☐ An interrogative pronoun is used to ask a question.

Interrogative pronouns: what   which   who

whom   whose

☐ A demonstrative pronoun points out one or more persons, places or things.

Demonstrative pronouns: this   these   that   those

☐ A relative pronoun connects a noun or pronoun with a group of words that tells more about it.

Relative pronouns: who   whom   whose   that   which

Chapter Quiz

A. Complete these sentences with a word from the box. Write the sentences on a separate sheet of paper.

relative	interrogative	demonstrative

1. An _____ pronoun is used to ask a question.

2. Pronouns that point out people, places, and things are called _____ pronouns.

3. A _____ pronoun connects a noun or pronoun with words that tell more about it.

B. Write the pronouns from these sentences on a separate sheet of paper. Write **I** after interrogative pronouns. Write **D** after demonstrative pronouns. Write **R** after relative pronouns.

1. What did Helen eat for dinner?

2. That is the man whom you called last week.

3. Which is your friend who works in the bank?

4. The bicycle that broke was new.

C. Complete these sentences with a demonstrative, relative, or interrogative pronoun of your own. Write the sentences on a separate sheet of paper.

1. "_____," asked the famous detective, "is the murderer?"

2. "From _____ did you get the most important clue?" he asked.

3. We all remembered the mysterious package _____ had arrived on Saturday night.

4. _____ of the people in the house had opened it?

5. _____ had been in it?

Unit Review

A. Find the pronouns in these sentences. Write them on a separate sheet of paper.

1. She is mowing her lawn herself.

2. I was surprised when they called us.

3. They pride themselves on being prompt.

4. Are these yours?

5. Her lizard can change its color.

6. Anything is possible if one just tries.

7. Both are acceptable to me.

B. Complete these sentences with pronouns of your own. Write the sentences on a separate sheet of paper.

1. Joe lost _____ keys.

2. _____ did Lois invite?

3. Fred and Janet are rehearsing _____ song.

4. Sara will come to the meeting with _____ .

5. Please wash the dishes and dry _____ .

6. Todd thinks _____ own is best.

7. Roberta rang, but _____ answered.

C. Use each pronoun in the box below in a sentence of your own. Write the sentences on a separate sheet of paper.

he	herself	who	which	them	its
that	they	we	someone	these	

Unit Four

Verbs

Chapter 7 Verb Forms

Look at the action in this photograph. What are these children doing? You need to use verbs to answer this question. Verbs are the words we use to express action.

Chapter Learning Objectives

Identify action verbs.

Identify linking verbs.

Use present tense verb forms.

Use past tense verb forms.

Use the forms of *be*.

Use the forms of *have*.

Use verbs in writing.

Words to Know

action verb a word that expresses physical or mental action

linking verb a word that expresses what is or what seems to be

past tense a verb form that shows action or being in the past

present tense a verb form that shows action or being in the present time

tense the time of the action or being expressed by a verb

verb a word that expresses action or being

Lesson 1: What Are Verbs?

A **verb** expresses an action or what is or seems to be.

Every sentence must have a verb.

Maureen **hit** the ball into the stands.

She **is** a new member of the team.

The pitcher **looks** puzzled.

Maureen **raced** around the bases.

She **became** a famous ball player.

Here's an easy way to identify verbs. Every sentence has a subject and a predicate. And the verb is always the predicate, or the most important part of the predicate. For example:
*Steve **drives**.*
*Steve **drives** a car.*

Practice 1

Find the verb in each of these sentences. Write the verbs on a separate sheet of paper. The first one is done for you.

1. Rick takes the bus to school.

   takes

2. The lion roared loudly.

3. Nadia and I are first cousins.

4. Snow fell late last night.

5. Tim exercises every day.

6. Those pears look delicious!

7. Both drivers stopped suddenly.

8. Sam is a wonderful cook.

9. Clem felt tired after the game.

10. Wanda looks unhappy this morning.

11. Jimmy read three books last week!

12. One of the books was about Napoleon!

13. Napoleon often rode a horse.

14. What was the color of Napoleon's white horse?

15. Roger knew the answer to that question.

A verb sometimes expresses an action that cannot be seen or heard.

Jerry **guessed** the answer.

Practice 2

Find the verbs in these sentences. Write them on a separate sheet of paper. The first one is done for you.

After people wake up in the morning, what do they do? Out of habit they usually do the same things every day. Describe the things you do each morning. You will need to use verbs.

1. Oliver misses his brother.

   misses

2. Sara decided on a blue shirt with long sleeves.

3. Mr. Ruben thought about the problem.

4. Paulina often dreams of traveling.

5. Everyone on the team wished for a home run.

A sentence can have two or more verbs.

> Joe **closed** the windows, **put** on his coat, and **went** outside.

Practice 3

Find the verbs in each of these sentences. Write them on a separate sheet of paper. The first sentence is done for you.

1. Patty sometimes turns on the radio and dances.

   turns dances

2. The dish slipped from Glen's hands and crashed to the floor.

3. Ms. Brown went to the phone, dialed a number, and spoke quietly.

4. They will read the chapter carefully and answer the questions.

5. Lynn woke up, jumped out of bed, and made coffee.

Practice 4

Complete each of these sentences with a verb of your own. Write the sentences on a separate sheet of paper.

1. Bob _____ a bird feeder for the yard.
2. Carla _____ a dollar on the stairs.
3. The group _____ a picnic.
4. Meg _____ several questions.
5. Rob and Marco _____ a cake for the party.

Lesson 2: Action Verbs

An **action verb** expresses a physical or mental action.

> He **told** an unbelievable story.
>
> Everyone **believed** the story.

Practice 1

Find the action verbs in these sentences. Write the verbs on a separate sheet of paper. The first one is done for you.

1. We swim in the lake each summer.

   swim

2. Sheila never judges other people.
3. Bob drives to his office in the city each day.
4. The plane landed safely during the snowstorm.
5. Hank eats a balanced diet.

6. The council considered the plan with care.

7. Those birds fly south in the winter.

8. They typed their term papers.

9. Tara always jogs on the beach at sunset.

10. The weather bureau predicts rain for tomorrow.

Practice 2

Complete each of these sentences on a separate sheet of paper. Use an action verb from the box. The first one is done for you.

worked	planned	slid	imagined
delivered	skipped	picked	purchased
ordered	rushed	played	built

1. Vito _____ a new stereo.

Vito purchased a new stereo.

2. We _____ a big surprise for Lauren.

3. Betty _____ into the room.

4. Gil _____ a huge chocolate cake.

5. I _____ until midnight.

6. Randy's puppy _____ across the ice.

7. They _____ a sand castle.

8. Irene _____ an interesting speech.

9. Some of us _____ wild blueberries.

10. Mr. Lee _____ his guitar.

to the Wise

Lesson 3: Linking Verbs

A **linking verb** expresses what **is** or what **seems to be**. It links the subject of a sentence with a word that describes it.

> Jerry **is** our friend.

Our friend describes the subject, Jerry.

> He always **looks** happy.

Happy describes how the subject (he) looks.

Be is the most common linking verb. The forms of **be** are **am, is, are, was,** and **were**.

Many linking verbs can also be action verbs. It depends on how they are used in the sentence:
Linking: *I looked sad.*
Action: *I looked at it.*

Other Common Linking Verbs			
Each of these verbs can be used as linking verbs.			
act	feel	remain	sound
appear	grow	seem	stay
become	look	smell	taste

Practice 1

Find the linking verbs in these sentences. Write the verbs on a separate sheet of paper. The first one is done for you.

1. Emily is a fine actress.

   is

2. They remained quiet throughout the performance.

3. The potatoes taste salty.

4. Suddenly Sean grew quiet.

5. Fran and Ned are excellent workers.

6. Little by little, the sky became cloudy.

7. That sounds wise to me.

8. Ray was captain of the team.

9. The dinner smells wonderful.

10. Linda appears calm.

Practice 2

Complete these sentences on a separate sheet of paper. Use a form of **be** or a linking verb from the box on page 114. The first one is done for you.

1. They sometimes _____ funny.

   They sometimes look funny.

2. Those cookies _____ delicious.

3. I never _____ bored.

4. The party guests _____ happy.

5. You _____ rather sad today.

6. They _____ the first people to finish.

7. These flowers _____ sweet.

8. The telephone call _____ for Dennis.

Lesson 4: Present Tense Verb Forms

A verb changes form to show present and past time. The time shown by a verb is called its **tense**.

The **present tense** shows action or being in the present. The present tense can also show repeated action.

☐ Action in the present: The cat **hides** under the sofa.

☐ Repeated action: The cat **hides** there whenever the dog **comes** into the room.

Practice 1

Find the present tense verbs in these sentences. Write the verbs on a separate sheet of paper. The first one is done for you.

1. They often camp in the woods.

   camp

2. The whistle blows at five o'clock.

3. Greg makes the greatest tacos in the world.

4. Those flowers only bloom in the spring.

5. She studies in her room every afternoon.

Most verbs have a singular and a plural present tense form.

The singular form ends with **-s**. This form goes with singular noun subjects and with the pronoun subjects **he, she,** and **it**.

Subjects	Verb Forms
The dog	**runs.**
He (she, it)	**runs.**

The plural form goes with plural noun subjects and with the pronoun subjects **I, you, we,** and **they**.

Subjects	Verb Forms
The dogs	**run.**
I (you, we, they)	**run.**

Practice 2

Rewrite these sentences on a separate sheet of paper. Choose the correct verb form in the parenthesis. The first one is done for you.

1. That band (perform, performs) at every assembly.

   That band performs at every assembly.

2. The cast (play, plays) several roles each.
3. Our family (spend, spends) holidays in Seattle.
4. The jury (argue, argues) over every point.
5. A huge mob (fill, fills) the street.

Use a singular verb with a singular indefinite pronoun. Use a plural verb with a plural indefinite pronoun.

Indefinite pronouns do not refer to any particular person or thing. Look back at Chapter 5 if you need to refresh your memory.

Singular Indefinite Pronouns

another	everybody	nothing
anybody	everyone	one
anyone	everything	other
anything	neither	somebody
each	nobody	someone
either	no one	something

Plural Indefinite Pronouns

both	few	many	several

Practice 3

Use the correct form of the verb to complete each of these sentences. Write the sentences on a separate sheet of paper. The first one is done for you.

1. Many _____ to come. (want)

   Many want to come.

2. Each _____ her own opinion. (have)

3. Few _____ with the chairperson. (agree)

4. Nobody _____ ready. (feel)

5. Several _____ glad to leave. (be)

6. Both _____ Spanish well. (speak)

7. Neither _____ brussel sprouts. (like)

8. No one ever _____ to me. (listen)

9. Either _____ a fine choice. (be)

10. Few _____ hidden treasure. (find)

Some indefinite pronouns may be singular or plural. Use a singular verb when you mean a specific person **or** one person or thing. Use a plural verb when you mean more than one person or thing.

All of the play was dull.

(**All** refers to one play. Here **all** is singular.)

All of the plays were dull.

(**All** refers to more than one play. Here **all** is plural.)

Indefinite Pronouns That May Be Singular or Plural

all   any   most   none   some   such

Practice 4

Read each of these sentences. Notice how the indefinite pronoun has been used in each sentence. If the indefinite pronoun subject is singular, write **S**. If the subject is plural, write **P**. The first sentence is done for you.

1. Some of the characters are interesting.

   P

2. Any of that is inexpensive.

3. Most of the children write well.

4. All of the painters use bold brush strokes.

5. All of the cereal is gone.

A sentence may have two or more subjects. Usually, when the subjects are joined by **and**, use a plural verb form.

> Carmen and Rosalind **are** here.

Sometimes the subjects are joined by **or** or **nor**. In that case the verb form goes with the last noun or pronoun in the subject.

> Either the pens or the pencils **are** on the table.

> Neither the pens nor the pencil **is** on the table.

Practice 5

Use the correct form of the verb to complete each sentence. Write the sentences on a separate sheet of paper. The first one is done for you.

1. Stan and Alex _____ brilliantly. (skate)

   Stan and Alex skate brilliantly.

2. Neither my cat nor my dog _____ in the house. (sleep)

3. The blue shoes and the red shoes _____ my feet. (hurt)

4. Either Ellie or her friends _____ every week. (call)

5. Some mittens or a hat _____ a useful gift. (make)

Use a singular verb form with the title of a book or movie. Use a singular verb form with the name of an organization or country.

> *Space Pioneers* **is** my favorite movie.

> The Philippines **is** an interesting country.

> The United Nations **meets** here.

Practice 6

Use the correct form of the verb to complete each sentence. Write the sentences on a separate sheet of paper. The first one is done for you.

1. The Friends of the Library _____ to raise money. (plan)

   The Friends of the Library plans to raise money.

2. The United States _____ to sign that agreement. (want)

3. *Great Trials* _____ a series of stories about five trials. (be)

4. *King Solomon's Mines* _____ on television again. (be)

5. *Pride and Prejudice* _____ Mona's favorite novel. (be)

6. The Red Cross _____ people when disaster strikes. (help)

7. *War and Peace* _____ the longest book I have ever read. (be)

8. China _____ more people than any other country. (have)

When you think of an amount as a single unit, use a singular verb form. When you think of an amount as individual units, use a plural verb form.

> One-third of the town **is** destroyed.
>
> One-third of the buildings **are** destroyed.

Practice 7

Think of each amount in these sentences as a single unit. Complete the sentences on a separate sheet of paper with the correct form of the verb. The first one is done for you.

1. Two-thirds of the football team _____ the flu. (have)

   Two-thirds of the football team has the flu.

2. Twenty-five dollars _____ too much for that. (be)

3. Three weeks _____ quickly if you are busy. (pass)

4. One-half of the fleet _____ into the harbor. (sail)

5. More than three-fourths of the forest _____ birch trees. (be)

Practice 8

Think of each amount in the following sentences as individual units. Complete the sentences on a separate sheet of paper. The first one is done for you.

1. One-half of the women _____ every day. (help)

   One-half of the women help every day.

2. Nine trucks _____ slowly up the mountain. (move)

3. Five of the six projects _____ completed. (be)

4. More than twelve of the cars _____ repairs. (need)

5. At least three of my favorite films _____ playing this week. (be)

Lesson 5: Past Tense Verb Forms

Past tense verb forms show action or being in the past. Many past tense verb forms are made by adding **-d** or **-ed** to the present tense plural form.

Present Tense Plural	Past Tense
Today they **work** hard.	Yesterday they **worked** hard.
	Yesterday I **worked** hard.

Practice 1

Find the past tense verb forms in these sentences. Write them on a separate sheet of paper. The first one is done for you.

1. The news shocked the nation.

   shocked

2. She photographed many famous people.

3. We arrived early.

4. Simon stayed for three hours.

5. He talked about nothing but Simon all that time.

6. I invited him.

7. They danced for hours.

8. The show started with a song.

9. Heather noticed the new guest.

10. Martin asked a difficult question.

Practice 2

Some of these sentences have past tense verb forms. Some have present tense forms. On a separate sheet of paper, copy only the sentences with past tense verb forms.

1. Pioneers crossed the country in covered wagons.
2. Lightning flashed during the storm.
3. The storm ended suddenly.
4. We often see lightning in this part of the country.
5. The show started with a song.
6. A family of birds once nested in that tree.
7. Howard asked his mother for the car.
8. Henry works for that company.
9. Ingrid started the discussion.
10. We watch every tennis match on television.

Practice 3

Complete each of these sentences on a separate sheet of paper with past tense verb forms of your own. The first one is done for you.

1. I _____ at each of her jokes.
   I laughed at each of her jokes.
2. Carol _____ that her jokes were funny.
3. But Carol's mother _____ that Carol should get serious.
4. She _____ Carol to get a job in an office.
5. Mr. Pringle _____ to hire Carol.

Lesson 6: Irregular Past Tense Verb Forms

Not all verbs form the past tense by adding **-d** or **-ed**. Some form the past tense in other ways. These are called irregular verbs. Some common irregular verbs are in the box below.

Present Plural	Past	Present Plural	Past
eat	ate	know	knew
give	gave	grow	grew
lie	lay	blow	blew
come	came	throw	threw
run	ran	fly	flew
begin	began	choose	chose
drink	drank	burst	burst
ring	rang	do	did
shrink	shrank	freeze	froze
swim	swam	speak	spoke
steal	stole	fall	fell
tear	tore	go	went
wear	wore	see	saw
take	took	drive	drove

Practice 1

Find the 13 irregular past tense verbs in these sentences. Write them on a separate sheet of paper. Some sentences have more than one irregular verb. The first one is done for you.

1. She wore a flower in her hair.

   wore

2. The race began when the bell rang.

3. Snow fell, and the pipes froze.

4. Only Mike knew which one they chose.

5. Sally smiled and spoke in a calm voice.

6. We dove into the pool and swam.

7. Kay saw who took the bracelet.

8. Jenny went home.

Practice 2

Complete these sentences on a separate sheet of paper. Use the past tense of the verb form. The first one is done for you.

1. The student (come) into the class.

   The student came into the class.

2. We (eat) cookies and (drink) milk.

3. The plane (fly) them directly to Washington.

4. Terry (see) what Michael (do).

5. My best sweater (shrink) in the wash.

Practice 3

Complete the sentences below on a separate sheet of paper. Use an irregular past tense verb from the box. The first one is done for you.

ate	shrank	grew	burst
gave	swam	blew	rang
lay	stole	threw	saw
came	tore	flew	went
ran	wore	chose	spoke
began	took	froze	drove
drank	knew	did	fell

1. Lee _____ the movie.

   Lee saw the movie.

2. I _____ it.

3. The bag was so full that it _____ .

4. Nanette _____ out the candles on her cake.

5. Dave _____ how fast Sue _____ .

6. That player _____ two bases.

7. The tired dog _____ down in the grass.

8. Is it true that Gary _____ all the juice?

9. You just _____ me a good idea.

10. Marsha and Frank _____ into town.

Chapter Review

Chapter Summary

☐ A verb is a word that expresses an action or a condition of being.

Verbs: jumps have be seem

☐ An action verb expresses a physical or a mental action.

Action verbs: write play think

☐ A linking verb expresses what is or what seems to be. A linking verb joins the subject of a sentence with a word that describes it.

Linking verbs: be seem

☐ The tense of a verb gives the time of a particular action or state of being. A present tense verb form shows action or being in the present. A past tense verb form shows action or being in the past.

Present tense verb forms: walk drive is

Past tense verb forms: walked drove was

☐ Most past tense verb forms are regular. They form the past by adding **-d** or **-ed** to the present plural verb form.

Regular past tense verb form: jumped

☐ Some verbs form the past tense in different ways. These verbs are called irregular verbs.

Irregular verb: saw

Chapter Quiz

A. Complete the sentences below on a separate sheet of paper. Use the correct word or word group from the box.

verb	irregular	action	past tense
linking		present tense	

1. A _____ verb states action or being in the present.

2. Most verbs have singular and plural _____ forms.

3. An _____ verb states physical or mental action.

4. A _____ verb states what is or seems to be.

5. A _____ verb states action or being in the past.

6. An _____ verb does not form the past tense by adding **-d** or **-ed.**

B. Write the verbs from these sentences on a separate sheet of paper. If a verb is in the past tense, write **past** next to it. If a verb is in the present tense, write **present**. Next to the present tense verbs, also write **S** for singular or **P** for plural.

1. That is a popular show.

2. Jan served carrots and zucchini.

3. The group comes to our house every Tuesday.

4. Neither Karen nor Ian liked public speaking.

C. On a separate sheet of paper, complete each sentence with a present or past tense verb form of your own.

1. *Kind Hearts and Coronets* _____ still funny today.

2. Everyone _____ to come.

3. Kim and Dana _____ skating.

4. The Kimballs seldom _____ us.

Chapter *8* Verb Phrases

Look at the people in the photograph. Notice how one person is helping the other. You will need to use verbs to describe what is happening. You may even have to use helping verbs to make your meaning clearer.

Chapter Learning Objectives

Identify verb phrases.

Explain the difference between helping and main verbs.

Use the helping verb *be* to form the present participle.

Use the helping verb *have* to form the past participle.

Use the words *will* and *shall* to form the future tense.

Explain the difference between active and passive voice.

Words to Know

active voice   the form of a verb that indicates the action is performed by the subject of a sentence

future tense   a verb form that shows action that will occur in the future. It is formed by using the words **will** or **shall** with a plural verb form.

helping verb   the verb in a verb phrase that helps the main verb tell what happens or what is

main verb   the verb in a verb phrase that tells what happens or what is

passive voice   the form of a verb that indicates the action is performed upon the subject of a sentence

past participle   a form of a verb usually made by adding **d, ed, n,** or **en** to the plural verb form

present participle   a form of a verb usually made by adding **ing** to the plural verb form

verb phrase   a phrase made up of one or more helping verbs and a main verb

Lesson 1: Verb Phrases with *Be*

A **verb phrase** is made up of one or more **helping verbs** and a **main verb**. The helping verb in a verb phrase is often a form of the verb **be**. For example:

Tom **is speaking**.

Verb phrase: is speaking

Helping verb: is

Main verb: speaking

The main verb in a verb phrase is often the **present participle**.

A present participle always follows a form of the helping verb **be**. The present participle is formed by adding **ing** to the plural form of the verb. Usually, if the plural form ends with **-e**, drop the **e** before adding **ing**.

Verb Phrases			
Helping Verb	Main Verb	Helping Verb	Main Verb
am	drawing	was	looking
is	writing	were	coming
are	thinking		

Remember that the subject of the sentence has to agree with the helping verb. For example, the word I must go with am, *as in "I am drawing."*

Verb phrases that use **am, is,** or **are** and a present participle tell of continuing action in the present. Verb phrases that use **was** or **were** and a present participle tell of continuing action in the past.

Practice 1

Find the verb phrase in each sentence. Write the verb phrases on a separate sheet of paper. The first one is done for you.

1. The bread was rising in the oven.

   was rising

2. I am hoping for a call from my friends.

3. All the leaves were changing colors.

4. We are planning a trip to Chicago.

5. Arthur and Bev are decorating for the party.

Practice 2

Change the verb in the parenthesis to a verb phrase. The verb phrase should show action continuing in the present. The first sentence is done for you.

1. Pedro (go) to the gym.

   Pedro is going to the gym.

2. You (gain) strength daily.

3. The thunder (get) louder.

4. They (watch) a movie on television.

5. It (become) a serious problem.

6. Corrine (look) for an apartment.

Lesson 2: Verb Phrases with *Have*

Have, has, and **had** are forms of the verb **have**. They are often used as helping verbs in a verb phrase.

The helping verb **have** is followed by a **past participle** in a verb phrase. The past participle is the main verb. A past participle is formed by adding **d, ed, n,** or **en** to the plural form of the verb.

   Tom **has spoken**.

Verb phrase: has spoken

Helping verb: has

Main verb: spoken

Practice 1

Find the verb phrases in these sentences. Write the verb phrases on a separate sheet of paper. The first one is done for you.

1. They have asked an important question.

   have asked

2. The child had fallen off her horse.
3. We have known them for three years.
4. The clerk has added up the figures.
5. Will and Wendy have spoken to the manager.
6. Pilar had tossed the paper in the waste basket.
7. Fortunately, Grant saved us seats.
8. Melissa had driven all night to get here.

Practice 2

Rewrite these sentences on a separate sheet of paper. Change the verb in the parenthesis to a verb phrase. Use **have** or **has** and the past participle. The first sentence is done for you.

1. We (give) several suggestions.

   We have given several suggestions.

2. No one (waste) any time.
3. The brave rescue workers (risk) their lives.
4. Their baby (grow) a lot in the past few weeks.
5. The audience (applaud) each diver.
6. Who (bake) those wonderful cupcakes?

Challenge

Find the verb phrase in the following sentence: I have had to have help.

Lesson 3: Verb Phrases with *Do*

Do and **does** are present tense forms of the verb **do**. **Did** is the past tense form. A form of **do** is sometimes used as a helping verb in a verb phrase. The main verb follows **do**. It is always a plural verb form.

The forms of **do** have three main uses.

☐ In questions:
"Do you like baseball?" asked Tod.

☐ With the word **not**:
"I do not like baseball," answered Tim.

☐ For emphasis:
"I do like baseball," insisted Terry.

Challenge

Sometimes, another word will come between a helping verb and a main verb in a verb phrase. Don't be confused by this! The verb phrase hasn't disappeared. For example, "Do you like" looks different than the verb phrase "do like." But it's the same verb phrase, even though the pronoun **you** comes between **do** and **like**. Now find the verb phrase in this sentence: **Does he like baseball?**

Practice 1

Rewrite these sentences on a separate sheet of paper. Draw a line under each verb phrase. The first one is done for you.

1. We did see it happen.

   We <u>did see</u> it happen.

2. Did it rain last night?

3. We do agree with them.

4. They do talk a lot!

5. Rachel does enjoy sports.

6. Those oranges do contain a lot of juice.

7. Did Doug tell you that?

8. They really do have interesting ideas.

9. What do you think is the matter?

10. Nobody does agree with his plan.

Practice 2

Change each of these sentences into questions. Use only the words in the sentence. Write the questions on a separate sheet of paper. The first one is done for you.

1. They do like baseball.

   Do they like baseball?

2. Sandra did have a good time on her vacation.

3. Elliot does know how to drive.

4. You do exercise regularly.

5. It does matter to Marsha.

Lesson 4: Verb Phrases and *Not*

The word **not** changes the meaning of a sentence. **Not** usually comes between the words in a verb phrase. **Not** is not part of the verb phrase. **Not** is a part of speech called an **adverb**. You will learn more about adverbs in Chapter 11.

> They will come
>
> Bill is expecting them.
>
> They will not come.
>
> Bill is not expecting them.

Practice 1

Copy these sentences on a separate sheet of paper. Draw a line under the verb phrase. The first one is done for you.

1. We did not watch that program.
   We <u>did</u> not <u>watch</u> that program.

2. Seth has not blown out the candles.
3. They had not prepared well enough.
4. Fern has not eaten yet.
5. Li did not read that book.
6. We are not beginning until ten.
7. Steven was not asking a huge favor.
8. The men have not finished their work.
9. The judges have not yet selected a winner.
10. Nobody ever did tell Harry.

Practice 2

Rewrite these sentences on a separate sheet of paper. Change each sentence by adding **not**. The first one is done for you.

1. Who has practiced her speech?
   Who has not practiced her speech?

2. The suspect did confess.
3. Carey was laughing at Pat's joke.
4. The meeting had started on time.
5. I had given up!
6. The detective does ask many questions.
7. Which one has broken?

Words to the Wise

People who live in glass houses should not throw stones.

Write this proverb on a separate sheet of paper. Draw a line under the verb phrase. Remember that a proverb states a truth or gives advice. Explain what this proverb means in your own words. Tell whether or not you agree with the proverb's message.

Hint: Would **you** want everyone to see what goes on in your house? Why not?

Lesson 5: Future Tense

A verb phrase with a present participle can show continuing action in the future. For example: I will be helpful.

The **future tense** tells of action or being in the future. To make the future tense, use a verb phrase with **will** or **shall** and a plural verb form.

I **shall help.**	We **shall help.**
I **will help.**	We **will help.**
He, She, It **will help.**	They **will help.**

Practice 1

Find the verb phrase in each of the sentences. Write the verb phrases on a separate sheet of paper. The first one is done for you.

1. Gerta will buy drawing paper.

   will buy

2. After the game, we shall celebrate our victory.

3. The hours till then will pass quickly.

4. Perhaps Bobbie and Irma will show us their slides.

5. In case of danger, a warning whistle will sound.

6. Gary will relax at home this weekend.

7. It will stop soon.

8. They will approach the problem with open minds.

Practice 2

Read each sentence. If the sentence tells about something that happened in the past, write **past**. If the sentence tells about something that is happening in the present, write **present**. If the sentence tells about something that will happen in the future, write **future**. Use a separate sheet of paper for your answers. The first one is done for you.

1. Some day I shall learn gymnastics.

   future

2. Before the test, Gordon studied hard.

3. You will not be sorry.

4. Last week the Jepsons cleaned out their garage.

5. By the end of the year, they will move.

6. It occurred to her too late.

7. Barry enjoys all sports.

8. He was on the baseball team last year

9. Now he plays tennis every day.

10. Is there any sport he does not play well?

Lesson 6: Other Helping Verbs

Other helping verbs are sometimes used in verb phrases. These helping verbs change the meaning of the sentence.

The helping verbs **can, could, may, might, must, should**, and **would** are followed by a plural verb form.

Read the sentences in the box. Think about what they mean.

	They sing.	might	They **might** sing.
can	They **can** sing.	must	They **must** sing.
could	They **could** sing.	should	They **should** sing.
may	They **may** sing.	would	They **would** sing.

Practice 1

Find the verb phrase in each of these sentences. Write the verb phrase on a separate sheet of paper. The first one is done for you.

1. I could wear my purple jumpsuit.

    could wear

2. Maybe we should eat a more balanced diet.
3. Singers must breathe properly.
4. It might explode!
5. Possums can hang by their tails.
6. Don should study harder.
7. He must pass this course.

Practice 2

Rewrite these sentences on a separate sheet of paper. Change the verb into a verb phrase. Use one of the helping verbs in the box on page 141 and the plural form of the verb. The first one is done for you.

1. Insects (destroy) plants.

   Insects can destroy plants.

2. With luck, there (be) a rainbow after the storm.

3. Our neighbors (lower) their stereo.

4. You know, I (change) my mind.

5. Everyone (prepare) a dish from his or her native land.

Lesson 7: Passive Verb Phrases

Up to now you have studied sentences in which the subject performs an action. Verbs in these sentences are in the **active voice.**

> The Living Daylights **gave** a concert.

> They **will give** another concert.

Sentences in which an action is done **to** the subject have verbs in the **passive voice.** These sentences always need a verb phrase.

> A concert **was given** by The Living Daylights.

> Another concert **will be given** by them.

To make the passive voice, use a form of **be** and a past participle.

Practice 1

Read the following sentences. Then number a sheet of paper from 1 to 5. Write the letter of the sentence with the verb phrase in the passive voice next to each number. The first one is done for you.

1. a. Leroy brought the pretzels.

   b. The pretzels were brought by Leroy.

   1. b

2. a. Traffic was slowed by heavy rain.

   b. Heavy rain slowed the traffic.

3. a. William Hudson wrote *Green Mansions*.

   b. *Green Mansions* was written by William Hudson.

4. a. The events were reported by Nat and Madge.

   b. Nat and Madge reported the events.

5. a. Tiny made the highest score.

   b. The highest score was made by Tiny.

Practice 2

Rewrite these sentences on a separate sheet of paper. Change the verb phrases to the passive voice. The first one is done for you.

1. No one witnessed the accident.

   The accident was witnessed by no one.

2. Snowplows cleared the roads.

3. Leslie knitted all those sweaters.

4. All had a good time!

Chapter Review

Chapter Summary

☐ The verb phrase in a sentence is made up of one or more helping verbs and a main verb.

Verb phrase: could win could have won

☐ The main verb in a verb phrase tells what happens or what is.

Main verb: win

☐ The helping verb in a verb phrase helps the main verb tell what happens or what is.

Helping verb: could

☐ A verb phrase may include a present participle. A verb phrase with a present participle is used to show continuing action in the past or present.

Present participle: working

Continuing action in the present: is working

Continuing action in the past: was working

Continuing action in the future: will be working

☐ A verb phrase may include a past participle.

Past participles: worked driven

Verb phrase: have worked had driven

☐ The future tense tells about action or being in the future.

Future tense: will win

☐ When the action is performed by the subject, the verb is in the active voice.

Active voice: Darlene **led** the group.

☐ When the action is performed on the subject, the verb is in the passive voice.

Passive voice: The group **was led** by Darlene.

Chapter Quiz

A. Use words from the box to complete these sentences on a separate sheet of paper.

verb phrase	present participle	past participle
future tense	main verb	helping verb

1. The _____ tells of action or being in the future.

2. The _____ is made by adding **d, ed, n,** or **en** to the plural verb form.

3. The _____ helps the main verb tell what happens or what is.

4. The _____ tells of continuing action in the past, present, or future.

5. The _____ tells what happens or what is.

6. A _____ is made up of one or more helping verbs and a main verb.

B. Write the verb phrases from these sentences on a separate sheet of paper. Write **H** above each helping verb. Write **M** above each main verb.

1. Penguins do not fly.

2. Who has crossed her name off the list?

3. We did attend the concert.

4. Charlene must not suspect our surprise.

5. We have seen him recently.

6. Every student must come.

7. Hilda could not answer the telephone.

Chapter 9 Verbs and Sentence Patterns

Look at the picture. Notice how the man hammers a nail into the wood. The nail *is receiving the action of the verb* hammers. *So* nail *is a* direct object. *In this chapter you will learn more about objects.*

Chapter Learning Objectives

Identify the simple subject.

Identify the simple predicate.

Use direct objects.

Use indirect objects.

Use object complements.

Use predicate nominatives.

Words to Know

direct object   a noun or pronoun that receives the action of a verb

indirect object   a noun or pronoun to whom or for whom an action is done

object complement   a noun or adjective that follows the direct object and refers back to it

predicate nominative   a noun or pronoun that follows a linking verb or verb phrase. The predicate nominative renames the subject noun or pronoun

simple predicate   the verb or verb phrase of a sentence

simple subject   the subject noun or pronoun of a sentence

Lesson 1: Simple Subject and Simple Predicate

You've already learned that the subject tells who or what the sentence is about. The **simple subject** is the part of the subject that is a noun or pronoun. So the simple subject is the subject noun or pronoun of a sentence.

The entire graduating class stood up and cheered.

Subject: The entire graduating class

Simple subject: class

The predicate tells what the subject does or is. The **simple predicate** is the part of the predicate that is a verb or verb phrase. So the simple predicate is the verb or verb phrase of a sentence.

They applauded wildly for five minutes.

Predicate: applauded wildly for five minutes

Simple predicate: applauded

All had listened carefully to the speech.

Predicate: had listened carefully to the speech

Simple predicate: had listened

Practice 1

Copy these sentences on a separate sheet of paper. Draw one line under the simple subject. Draw two lines under the simple predicate. The first one has been done for you.

You probably remember that a sentence can have several nouns or pronouns. In Practice 1, many of the sentences have nouns in addition to the subject *noun or pronoun.*

1. The happy group prepared a delicious dinner.
   The happy <u>group</u> <u>prepared</u> a delicious dinner.

2. The foolish boy swam rapidly away from the shore.

3. A bright sun rose over the tall trees.

4. The small mouse ran quickly across the field.

5. The mascot for our team is a terrier.

6. Several young women walked into the room.

7. They explained the report in detail.

8. The response to the play was outstanding.

9. Each actor bowed deeply.

10. Nobody in the room heard either talk.

Practice 2

Complete each sentence with a simple subject of your own. Write the sentences on a separate sheet of paper. The first one is done for you.

1. _____ announced the start of the race.
   A gunshot announced the start of the race.

2. _____ ran around the field.

3. _____ arrived at the finish line.

4. _____ was declared the winner.

5. _____ fell down.

6. _____ presented the gold medal.

7. _____ watched the presentations.

8. _____ sang the national anthem.

9. _____ carried flowers to the winner.

10. _____ thanked everyone for the award.

Practice 3

Complete each sentence with a simple predicate of your own. Write the sentences on a separate sheet of paper. The first one has been done for you.

1. My friend Jack _____ me a book.
   My friend Jack gave me a book.

2. The tall man _____ loudly.

3. His sister May _____ several dresses.

4. Their family _____ him to go.

5. The storm _____ late in the evening.

6. His supervisor _____ him.

7. Everyone _____ the story.

8. The group at the shop _____ with Danny.

9. All of her friends _____ rock music.

10. Somebody _____ the diamonds.

Challenge

Make up a sentence of your own that has a simple subject and a simple predicate.

Lesson 2: Direct Objects

A **direct object** is the noun or pronoun that receives the action of a verb. A direct object comes after the verb or verb phrase. The object always follows an action verb. It never follows a linking verb.

Direct objects are a very important part of speech. Think about it. Without objects, we couldn't make dinner, buy presents, eat soup, or even wash dishes.

We made **dinner.**   We made **it.**

Clara bought **presents.**   Clara bought **them.**

We ate some of the **soup.** We ate some of **it.**

We washed the **dishes**.   We washed **them.**

Practice 1

Copy these sentences on a separate sheet of paper. Draw a line under each direct object. The first one is done for you.

1. Caroline bought food.

   Caroline bought <u>food</u>.

2. In her room she kept a photograph.

3. Mr. Kwang saw us.

4. Arturo and I found a kitten.

5. Who took my pad?

6. Jacqueline asked Sylvia.

7. We hung dozens of balloons.

8. Most Eskimos have never seen an igloo.

9. A cowboy's high boots protect him.

10. Helga has several cameras.

11. Shelley wanted to buy a typewriter.

12. We saw beautiful scenery on our trip.

Practice 2

Complete each sentence with a direct object noun of your own. Write the sentences on a separate sheet of paper. The first one has been done for you.

1. Kuan Li knows _____ well.

   Kuan Li knows Chinese well.

2. Amos looked at the _____ .

3. The store manager warned those _____ .

4. You helped many _____ .

5. Several people wanted this _____ .

6. Leo painted the _____ red.

7. Wendy threw the _____ in the garbage.

8. Phil fed the _____ .

9. Do you want to try on this _____ ?

10. The last time Tom went fishing, he caught a _____ .

A sentence may have more than one direct object.

Pilar bought **milk** and **bread.**

Practice 3

Copy these sentences on a separate sheet of paper. Draw a line under each direct object. The first one has been done for you.

1. Did Dotty order soup or salad?

   Did Dotty order <u>soup</u> or <u>salad</u>?

2. Donna has two dogs and a cat.

3. Bev wrote a letter and a post card.

4. Do you want to take a raincoat or an umbrella?

5. Mark visited New York and Boston.

Words to the Wise

Talk doesn't cook rice.

Write this proverb on a separate sheet of paper. Draw a line under the direct object. Remember that a proverb states a truth or gives advice. Explain what this proverb means in your own words.

Hint: Is this saying more about cooking or talking?

Other words are often added to sentences with direct objects. These words give more information about the direct object.

Morgan planted seeds.

Morgan planted **tomato** seeds **in the spring.**

Practice 4

Rewrite these sentences on a separate sheet of paper. Add words to give more information about the direct object. The first one has been done for you.

1. The man played songs.

    The man played sad songs on the piano.

2. They all enjoy music.

3. Mrs. Yamato grew roses.

4. Gwen likes dogs.

5. Suzanne found information.

Challenge

Use the word **car** in a sentence of your own. Make **car** the direct object of your sentence. Use words that give more information about the object.

The pronouns in the box can be used as direct objects.

| me | you | him | her | it | us | them |

Kyle saw **them**.   Nancy asked **him**.

Practice 5

Complete each sentence with a direct object pronoun of your own. Write the sentences on a separate sheet of paper. The first one has been done for you.

1. Pedro could not locate _____ .

   Pedro could not locate them.

2. Carl distributed _____ to the audience.

3. Anna took _____ home.

4. Tom met _____ at the supermarket.

5. Jim enjoyed _____ more.

6. Some of the people wanted _____ to speak.

Lesson 3: Indirect Objects

An **indirect object** is the noun or pronoun to whom or for whom an action was done.

An indirect object comes after the verb and before the direct object in a sentence.

An indirect object never comes after the words **for** or **to**.

> Gina gave the **dog food.**

indirect object: **dog**

direct object: **food**

The pronouns in the box can be used as indirect objects.

The same pronouns can be either direct or indirect objects. You can tell by how they are used in the sentence.

me	you	him	her	it	us	them

Notice that a sentence cannot have an indirect object unless it has a direct object.

Gina gave **him food.**

indirect object: **him**

direct object: **food**

Practice 1

Copy these sentences on a separate sheet of paper. Draw a line under each indirect object. Draw two lines under each direct object. The first one has been done for you.

   1. Chee lent you his car.

      Chee lent <u>you</u> his <u>car</u>.

   2. Carmen promised me some cookies.

   3. Stan and Gigi showed us the dance.

   4. Evelyn sent me a post card.

   5. Tina left you this note.

   6. Herman's grandfather told me the story.

   7. The doctor gave Billy a shot.

   8. Mrs. Ionesco asked Joe a question.

Practice 2

Complete each sentence with an indirect object of your own. Write the sentences on a separate sheet of paper. The first one has been done for you.

   1. Someone sent _____ a letter.

      Someone sent him a letter.

   2. Myra told _____ a joke.

   3. Roberto saved _____ money.

   4. Dr. Kahn showed _____ the report.

5. Mrs. Carson gave _____ the books.

6. The librarian wrote _____ a note.

Practice 3

Rewrite these sentences on a separate sheet of paper. Add words to give more information. The first one has been done for you.

1. Cory bought us groceries.

   Cory bought us two bags of groceries at Hogan's.

2. The store mailed him the bill.

3. Mr. Chu gave the landlord a check.

4. William told us a story.

5. Eddy gave us a present.

6. Harry showed us a picture.

Lesson 4: Object Complements

An **object complement** follows a direct object and refers back to it. An object complement renames or tells more about the direct object.

The club made **Henrietta president.**

direct object: **Henrietta**

object complement: **president**

President renames **Henrietta.**

She proved **herself capable.**

direct object: **herself**

object complement: **capable**

Capable tells more about **herself.**

Practice 1

Copy these sentences on a separate sheet of paper. Draw a line under each direct object. Draw two lines under each object complement. The first one has been done for you.

1. They found the house deserted.
   They found the house deserted.
2. That made Jeremy suspicious.
3. They thought the noises strange.
4. The visitors made themselves comfortable.
5. The voters elected him mayor.

Practice 2

Complete each sentence with an object complement of your own. Write the sentences on a separate sheet of paper. The first one is done for you.

1. I found the music _____ .
   I found the music beautiful.
2. He proved himself _____ .
3. They find computers _____ .
4. Some people consider her _____ .
5. Their company made the trip _____ .

Lesson 5: Predicate Nominatives

Name five linking verbs. Look back at Chapter 7 if you need help.

A **predicate nominative** is a noun or pronoun that renames the subject noun or pronoun. The predicate nominative follows a linking verb or verb phrase.

Lael is a **nurse.**

That is **he.**

Practice 1

Copy these sentences on a separate sheet of paper. Draw a line under each linking verb. Draw two lines under each predicate nominative. The first one has been done for you.

1. The president could be you.

   The president <u>could be</u> <u>you</u>.

2. Those people are voters.

3. They are applicants.

4. His gift was a scarf.

5. She may become a pilot.

6. Mr. Samuels is our teacher.

Practice 2

Complete each sentence with a predicate nominative of your own. Write the sentences on a separate sheet of paper. The first one has been done for you.

1. We may become _____ .

   We may become friends.

2. Some of us are _____ .

3. He will be _____ .

4. The winner is _____ .

5. Miss Hernandez became _____ .

6. Those animals could be _____ .

Practice 3

Rewrite these sentences on a separate sheet of paper. Add words to give more information about the predicate nominative. The first one has been done for you.

1. Sandra Jones is a candidate.

   Sandra Jones is a well qualified candidate for mayor.

2. We shall be employees.

3. My friend is the editor.

4. Dr. Jensen should be the leader.

5. They are veterans.

Chapter Review

Chapter Summary

☐ Every sentence has a simple subject and a simple predicate. The simple subject is the subject noun or pronoun. The simple predicate is the verb or verb phrase.

> **Simple subject:** A tall **man** in a blue suit arrived.

> **Simple predicate:** He **walked** slowly into the room.

☐ The direct object in a sentence is the noun or pronoun that receives the action of the verb or verb phrase.

> **Direct objects:** Cal hit the **ball.**

> Cal hit **it.**

☐ The indirect object is the noun or pronoun to whom or for whom an action was done.

> **Indirect objects:** I gave **Jerry** the letter.

> I gave **him** the letter.

☐ The object complement is a noun or pronoun that follows the direct object and refers back to it. The object complement renames or tells more about the direct object.

> **Object complements:** They appointed Lewis **director.**

> He considered it **exciting.**

☐ A predicate nominative renames the subject noun or pronoun. A predicate nominative follows a linking verb or verb phrase.

> **Predicate nominative:** Rick is a **singer.**

Chapter Quiz

A. Number a separate sheet of paper from 1 to 6. Match the words in Column A with their definitions in Column B. Write a letter next to each number.

A	B
1. direct object	a. the subject noun or pronoun of a sentence
2. simple subject	b. the verb or verb phrase of a sentence
3. predicate nominative	c. the noun or pronoun that receives the action of the verb or verb phrase
4. simple predicate	d. the noun or pronoun to whom or for whom an action is done
5. indirect object	e. a noun or pronoun that follows the direct object and refers back to it
6. object complement	f. a noun or pronoun that follows a linking verb or verb phrase and renames the subject noun or pronoun

B. Copy the underlined words or word groups on a separate sheet of paper. Next to each write whether it is a simple subject, simple predicate, direct object, or indirect object.

1. Grace <u>left</u> yesterday on a three-week trip.

2. Darin waxed the <u>floor</u> in the dining room.

3. Edith made <u>grandfather</u> a sweater.

4. The <u>house</u> with the green roof was sold.

5. Tell <u>him</u> the truth.

6. A small yellow <u>car</u> was parked in the driveway.

7. He told <u>me</u> about the problem.

8. She sent the <u>package</u> yesterday.

9. I <u>have seen</u> him many times.

Unit Review

A. Complete these sentences on a separate sheet of paper. Use the past tense of the verb form.

1. She (lie) on the couch and (take) a nap.

2. They (ring) the doorbell and (go) inside.

3. When he (fall), his shirt (tear).

4. Their business (grow) rapidly.

5. Harry (steal) a glance backward as he (run).

B. Rewrite these sentences on a separate sheet of paper. Change the meaning of each sentence by adding the word **not**.

1. Susan is sleeping at the moment.

2. Hanno did try to call.

3. Kim and Ann do agree.

4. He does think so.

5. Len did sell one car today.

C. Copy these sentences on a separate sheet of paper. Draw a line under each direct object. Draw two lines under each object complement.

1. We found that movie enjoyable.

2. She made the decision final.

3. Many people found the class difficult.

4. Carla found it easy.

5. The band appointed Robbie leader.

Unit Five

Adjectives and Adverbs

Chapter *10* **Adjectives**

Look carefully at the photograph. Choose an object in it that interests you. Think about how you would describe that object to someone who has not seen it. To do a good job, you would have to use words that give a clear picture. You would have to use adjectives. Adjectives are words that are used to describe a noun or a pronoun.

Chapter Learning Objectives

Identify adjectives.

Identify proper adjectives.

Use capital letters with proper adjectives.

Use adjectives to make comparisons.

Use exact adjectives.

Words to Know

adjective   a word that describes a noun or a pronoun. Adjectives usually tell what kind, which one, or how many.

articles   the adjectives **a, an,** and **the**

proper adjective   an adjective formed from a proper noun. Proper adjectives refer to the names of particular persons, places, things, events, and ideas.

Lesson 1: What Are Adjectives?

An **adjective** is a word that describes a noun or pronoun. Adjectives usually tell what kind, which one, or how many. Many times an adjective comes before a noun in a sentence.

The words in dark type are adjectives.

She bought **yellow** flowers.

Those flowers are in the vase.

There are **six** vases full.

Practice 1

Find the adjectives in these sentences. Write the adjectives on a separate sheet of paper. The first sentence is done for you.

1. Ancient Egyptians slept on hard pillows.

   Ancient, hard

2. Benjamin Franklin drew political cartoons.

3. Silver dollars were the first coins made here.

4. Male crickets produce more chirps in warm weather.

5. The life of an average fly lasts two weeks.

6. Rubber is an essential ingredient in this gum.

7. Giant tortoises can live for 2,000 years.

8. Black sheep have a better sense of smell than white sheep.

Practice 2

Complete these sentences with adjectives of your own. Write the sentences on a separate sheet of paper.

1. The _____ coat is in the closet.

2. It was a _____ sale at a _____ store.

3. _____ children started to cry.

4. The _____ cups are on the _____ counter.

Words to the Wise

A rolling stone gathers no moss.

Write this proverb on a separate sheet of paper. Draw a line under the adjective. Remember that a proverb is always about people. Explain what this saying means in your own words.

Lesson 2: Adjectives Before Nouns

All adjectives can come before nouns, but some adjectives **must** come before nouns. The adjectives in the box are only used before nouns.

a	each	most	that
an	either	neither	the
another	every	one	these
any	few	several	this
both	many	some	those

Three of the adjectives in the box have a special name. They are called **articles**. **A, an,** and **the** are articles.

Practice 1

On a separate sheet of paper write the adjectives from these sentences. Do not write the articles. Next to each adjective, write the noun it describes.

The first sentence is done for you.

1. *Romeo and Juliet* is a sad play.

   sad play

2. Alex Haley wrote a popular novel called *Roots*.

3. Many people saw an interesting production of it on television.

4. The *Taming of the Shrew* is a funny play.

5. The heroine is the independent Kate.

6. She has a fiery temper.

7. Kate is courted by the spirited Petruchio.

8. She makes an important speech at the end of the play.

9. Petruchio treats Kate as if she were a gentle lady.

10. Some stories have happy endings.

Challenge

Adjectives tell different kinds of things. Name three adjectives that tell about color. Name three adjectives that tell about size. Name three adjectives that tell how many.

Lesson 3: Adjectives After Linking Verbs

Adjectives can also come after a form of **be** or another linking verb. Such adjectives are called **predicate adjectives**. A predicate adjective tells about the noun or pronoun that is the subject of the sentence.

The flower is **red**.

In this sentence, the adjective **red** tells about the noun **flower**.

More than one adjective can tell about a noun.

The room was **bright** and **cheerful**.

In this sentence, the adjectives **bright** and **cheerful** tell about the noun **room**.

Practice 1

On a separate sheet of paper, write the adjectives from these sentences. Do not write the articles. Next to each adjective, write the noun it tells about. The first one is done for you.

1. The street was dark and deserted.

   dark street   deserted street

2. The man was alone.

3. He seemed frightened.

4. The noise was sudden and loud.

5. It seemed startling.

6. The restaurant looked inviting.

7. Ricky and Janice were late.

8. Service at the restaurant was good.

9. No one was surprised.

10. Selma might be angry with us.

Try this for fun!

Imagine that you are going on a blind date. You arrange to meet your date at a certain coffee shop. As the two of you speak on the phone, your date asks "How will I recognize you?" Go ahead and describe yourself. You will need to use adjectives!

Lesson 4: Proper Adjectives

Proper adjectives are formed from proper nouns. Proper adjectives refer to the names of particular persons, places, things, events, and ideas.

Proper adjectives begin with capital letters.

My **Hawaiian** shirt is missing.

The **Roman** myths are interesting.

Practice 1

On a separate sheet of paper write the proper adjectives from these sentences. Next to each proper adjective, write the noun it tells about. The first one is done for you.

1. Italian cooking is very popular in this country.

   Italian cooking

2. Neapolitan pizza is many people's favorite.

3. Edward Teller, an American scientist, was born in Hungary.

4. The Spanish explorers traveled far.

5. The Brazilian business people have arrived.

6. He spent all his Japanese money.

7. Cyclops was a one-eyed monster in Greek myths.

8. Shakespeare was an English writer.

9. *War and Peace* is the title of a Russian novel.

10. Claudine sang a French song.

Practice 2

Complete these sentences with proper adjectives. Write the sentences on a separate sheet of paper. The first one is done for you.

1. Have you tasted _____ olives?

   Have you tasted Greek olives?

2. George Washington was the first _____ president.

3. Do you like _____ food?

4. The author of that book is _____ .

5. He enjoys _____ music.

Lesson 5: Using Adjectives to Make Comparisons

Adjectives can be used to compare two or more people, places, things, events, or ideas.

Compare yourself to another person in your class. Think about how the two of you look and act. You will need to use adjectives ending in -er.

When you compare two, use the form of the adjective that ends with **-er**.

> The World Trade Center is taller than the Empire State Building.

When you compare more than two, use the form of the adjective that ends with **-est**.

> The World Trade Center is the tallest building in New York City.

Practice 1

Choose the correct form of the adjective in each sentence. Write these adjectives on a separate sheet of paper. The first one is done for you.

1. Nina's hair is (longer, longest) than Carrie's.

    longer

2. This room is the (bigger, biggest) in the house.
3. This is the (harder, hardest) job he has ever had.
4. My uncle is (older, oldest) than my mother.
5. This road is (steeper, steepest) than the other road.

Use **more** and **most** in comparisons with adjectives that have three or more syllables. Use **more** and **most** with some adjectives that have two syllables.

Use **more** when you are comparing two people or things.

Use **most** when you are comparing three or more people or things.

> I was **more** interested than he was.
>
> Jane was **more** eager to come than her sister.
>
> It was the **most** informative tour we had ever taken.

Practice 2

Rewrite these sentences on a separate sheet of paper. Use either **more** or **most** with the adjective. The first one is done for you.

1. Jed was (helpful) than Lewis.

    Jed was more helpful than Lewis.

2. A crocodile may be (dangerous) than a lion.

3. What is the (dangerous) animal in the world?

4. The (expensive) strawberries in the world cost $42 a piece.

5. Don is (responsible) than Steve.

6. A train tunnel was the scene of one of history's (terrible) accidents.

7. He was one of Hollywood's (successful) actors.

8. Which of the two watches is (accurate)?

9. That test was (difficult) than last week's.

10. Aspirin is still one of the (effective) painkillers.

Use **less** when you are comparing two things or people.

Use **least** when you are comparing three or more things or people.

> Your apartment is **less** bright than mine.
>
> Julie has the **least** bright apartment in the building.

Practice 3

Complete these sentences by adding **less** or **least**. Write the sentences on a separate sheet of paper. The first one is done for you.

1. Mandy was _____ tired than her brother.
   Mandy was less tired than her brother.

2. Sam was the _____ frightened of anyone in the room.

3. The amount was _____ than she expected.

4. Who is the _____ experienced?

5. She is _____ quiet than her sister.

The forms of the adjective **good** are **good, better, and best**.

Use **better** when comparing two.

Use **best** when comparing more than two.

> This movie is **better** than that one.

> It is the **best** movie I have ever seen.

The forms of the adjective **bad** are **bad, worse** and **worst**.

Use **worse** when comparing two.

Use **worst** when comparing more than two.

> This movie is **worse** than that one.

> It is the **worst** movie I have ever seen.

Practice 4

Rewrite these sentences on a separate sheet of paper. Use the correct form of the adjective. The first one is done for you.

1. This book is (good) than that one.

   This book is better than that one.

2. This is the (good) restaurant in the city.

3. My new apartment is (good) than my old.

4. It is the (bad) he has ever had.

5. It is even (bad) than the one he had last year.

Lesson 6: Spelling Adjectives Correctly

Some one-syllable adjectives end with a vowel followed by a consonant. Double the final consonant before you add **er** or **est** to these adjectives.

big	bigger	biggest	fat	fatter	fattest

Some adjectives end with a consonant followed by -**y**. Change the **y** to **i** before adding **er** or **est** to these adjectives.

dry	drier	driest	silly	sillier	silliest

Practice 1

Rewrite these sentences on a separate sheet of paper. Use the correct form of the adjective. The first one is done for you.

1. John was (angry) of all.
   John was angriest of all.

2. That joke was (silly) than the last one.

3. It is the (hot) day of the year.

4. This is the (heavy) piece of all the furniture.

5. The roads are (wet) today than they were yesterday.

6. This kitten has the (silky) fur of all.

7. This bear is (big) than that.

8. It is the (crazy) joke he has ever played.

Practice 2

Complete the sentences with adjectives of your own. Write the sentences on a separate sheet of paper.

1. The _____ man carried a _____ package.

2. Several _____ people spoke to their _____ boss.

3. The _____ house with the _____ yard was hard to sell.

4. A _____ chair and a _____ table were delivered today.

5. The office was _____ and _____ .

Lesson 7: Exact Adjectives

Imagine that you are telling a friend about a party you went to. Give your friend a clear picture of who was there and what it was like. Use exact adjectives.

You can make your writing clearer and more interesting by using exact adjectives.

Read these three sentences. Decide which sentence is the clearest and most interesting.

Flowers were in a vase on the table.

Nice flowers were in an **old** vase on the **unattractive** table.

Fresh yellow and **red** flowers were in a **cracked gray** vase on the **dusty** table.

The first sentence has no adjectives except the articles **a** and **the**. It doesn't give you a clear picture of the flowers on the table. Three adjectives in dark type have been added to the second sentence. They do not tell much. They are not exact adjectives. Exact adjectives have been added to the last sentence. That sentence gives the clearest picture.

Practice 1

Read each pair of adjectives. Decide which one in each pair gives the clearer picture. Write these adjectives on a separate sheet of paper. The first one is done for you.

1. bright, brilliant

   brilliant

2. exhausted, tired

3. soft, mushy

4. gritty, sandy

5. noisy, thunderous

6. loud, deafening

7. hot, feverish

8. glassy, smooth

9. large, gigantic

10. tasty, spicy

Practice 2

On a separate sheet of paper, write at least one exact adjective that could describe each of the following.

1. rain

2. the sun

3. the street you live on

4. ice cream

5. a supermarket

6. this room

Chapter Review

Chapter Summary

☐ An adjective is a word that describes a noun or pronoun. Adjectives usually tell what kind, which one, or how many.

Adjectives: pretty that three

The adjectives **a, an,** and **the** are called **articles.**

☐ A proper adjective is formed from a proper noun. Proper adjectives refer to the names of particular persons, places, things, events, and ideas. A proper adjective begins with a capital letter.

Proper adjective: American

Chapter Quiz

A. Rewrite these sentences on a separate sheet of paper. Fill in each blank with the correct word or word group from the box.

adjective	article	proper adjective

1. An _____ describes a noun or pronoun.

2. A _____ can refer to a particular place.

3. **An** is an _____ .

B. On a separate sheet of paper, write the adjectives from these sentences. Write **compares** next to adjectives that compare and **proper** next to adjectives that are formed from proper nouns. Notice that some sentences have more than one adjective.

1. More people drink coffee than tea.

2. Jose is stronger than George.

3. This is the worst cold I ever had.

4. I use less sugar than she does.

5. Most people like Mexican food.

6. Paul has a better idea about that.

7. Laverne is sweet and kind.

C. Choose the correct form of the adjective in each sentence. Write these adjectives on a separate sheet of paper.

1. What is the (taller, tallest) building you have ever visited?

2. Which of the two films is (longer, longest)?

3. April can be the (wetter, wettest) month of the year.

4. This package seems (lighter, lightest) than that one.

5. Apples are (sweeter, sweetest) than grapefruit.

Chapter *11* Adverbs

Look at the photograph. Describe what the people are doing. Use a verb to name each action. If you want to give a clearer picture of each action, you will have to use adverbs. Adverbs are words that tell how, where, when, or how many times an action takes place.

Chapter Learning Objectives

Identify and use adverbs.

Explain the difference between adjectives and adverbs.

Use adverbs to make comparisons.

Identify and avoid double negatives.

Use exact adverbs.

Words to Know

adverb   a word that tells more about a verb or verb phrase. An adverb tells how, where, when, or how many times something is done. Adverbs also modify adjectives or other adverbs.

contraction   a shortened form of a word or group of words in which an apostrophe takes the place of the missing letter or letters

negative   a word or phrase that expresses denial or says "no," such as **not**

Lesson 1: What Are Adverbs?

An **adverb** is a word that tells more about a verb or verb phrase. An adverb tells how, where, when, or how many times an action takes place.

☐ Adverb that tells how: She put up posters **quickly**.

☐ Adverb that tells where: She put up posters **everywhere**.

☐ Adverb that tells when: She put up posters **yesterday**.

☐ Adverb that tells how many times: She put up posters **twice**.

You use adverbs all the time. For example, think of something you did yesterday. Let's say you worked—at school or on the job. How did you work? Use adverbs in your answer.

Practice 1

Write the adverbs from these sentences on a separate sheet of paper. The first one is done for you.

1. The woman spoke loudly.

 loudly

2. Some birds can fly backwards.

3. Yo-yos were first used as weapons.

4. Robby wrapped the present slowly.

5. He folded the ends neatly.

6. He tied the bow carefully.

7. His little niece ripped open the package hastily.

8. She saw what was inside.

9. She yelled delightedly.

10. Once, the moon may have been part of the earth.

Practice 2

Write the adverbs from these sentences on a separate sheet of paper. Next to each adverb write how it is used in the sentence. If the adverb tells how an action was done write **how**. If the adverb tells where, write **where**. If the adverb tells when, write **when**. If the adverb tells how many times, write **how many**. The first one is done for you.

1. They will arrive tomorrow.

 tomorrow—when

2. Babe Ruth first became famous as a pitcher.

3. Later, he gained fame as a hitter.

4. Crowds cheered him wildly.

5. Both contestants stepped forward.

6. Murray drummed his fingers impatiently.

7. Kelly found this outside.

8. She did everything differently.

9. People often give Abner Doubleday credit for inventing baseball.

10. Others say Doubleday never played the game.

Words to the Wise

It never rains but it pours.

Write this proverb on a separate sheet of paper. Then draw a line under the adverb. Remember that a proverb states a truth or gives advice. Explain what this proverb means in your own words.

Hint: Does it ever seem to you that when one thing goes wrong, everything else seems to go wrong?

Lesson 2: Adverbs That Tell More About Adjectives

Some adverbs tell more about adjectives. These adverbs tell how much, how little, and to what degree.

That is a very powerful car. (**Very** tells **how powerful** the car is.)

It is too expensive for me. (**Too** tells **how expensive** it is.)

The engine is rather unsafe. (**Rather** tells **how unsafe** the engine is.)

Some adverbs that tell more about adjectives are in the box.

very	too	rather	fairly	truly
extremely		unusually		exceptionally
	somewhat		especially	

Practice 1

The adverbs in these sentences are used to tell more about adjectives. Write these adverbs on a separate sheet of paper. Next to each adverb, write the adjective it tells more about. The first one has been done for you.

1. It was fairly bright in the room.

   fairly—bright

2. Our dog can do some unusually difficult tricks.

3. We taught her at an especially early age.

4. Marvin woke up at a rather late hour.

5. Cynthia explained a truly difficult problem.

6. Sears Tower is an extremely tall building.

7. The Chinese system of writing is very complex.

8. She was an exceptionally popular singer.

9. The weather was somewhat cold.

10. It was too good to be true.

Lesson 3: Adverbs That Tell More About Other Adverbs

Some adverbs tell more about other adverbs. They tell how much, how little, how often, and to what degree.

Ted played fairly well. (**Fairly** tells **how** well.)

He hit the ball especially hard. (**Especially** tells **how hard.**)

Some adverbs that tell more about other adverbs are in the box.

Do the adverbs in the box look familiar? That's because they were in the box of adverbs in Lesson 2. As you can see, the same words can be used to describe both adjectives and adverbs.

very	too	rather	fairly	truly
extremely		unusually		exceptionally
	somewhat		especially	

Practice 1

Each of these sentences contains two adverbs. One of the adverbs tells more about the other adverb. Write the adverbs on a separate sheet of paper. Draw a line under the adverb that tells more about the other adverb. The first one is done for you.

1. The frightened child ran extremely quickly.

   <u>extremely</u> quickly

2. Cyril wants to go to the movies too often.

3. Selma cooked the meat exceptionally quickly.

4. Dan answered rather wearily.

5. Ann spoke very happily about her vacation.

6. Kyle lives truly comfortably in that small house.

7. Wendy spoke fairly briefly.

Practice 2

Complete these sentences with an adverb that tells more about the adverb given. Write the sentences on a separate sheet of paper. The first one has been done for you.

1. Sara worked _____ quickly.
   Sara worked unusually quickly.

2. Someone said the dogs were barking _____ loudly.

3. The writer finished the report _____ quickly.

4. Ken read it _____ eagerly.

5. The race finished _____ slowly.

6. The judges worked _____ carefully.

7. I like to read interesting books _____ often.

8. The first contestant stepped _____ slowly onto the stage.

9. For some minutes, he stared _____ nervously at the audience.

10. When he began to sing, he sang _____ well.

Lesson 4: Knowing When to Use Adjectives and Adverbs

Use adjectives to tell more about nouns and pronouns.

> His **voice** was **loud**.
>
> **He** was **angry**.

☐ Adjective: **loud**   Noun: **voice**

☐ Adjective: **angry**   Pronoun: **He**

Use adverbs to tell more about verbs and verb phrases, adjectives, and adverbs.

> The man **spoke loudly**.

- ☐ Adverb: **loudly**   Verb: **spoke**

> The man **had spoken loudly.**

- ☐ Adverb: **loudly**   Verb phrase: **had spoken**

> The sky was **very dark.**

- ☐ Adverb: **very**   Adjective: **dark**

> The man spoke **quite loudly.**

- ☐ Adverb: **quite**   Adverb: **loudly**

Use the adjective **good** to tell more about a noun or pronoun.

Use the adverb **well** to tell more about a verb or verb phrase.

> Roger has a **good** car.

> He **drives** it **well**.

- ☐ Adjective: **good**   Noun: **car**

- ☐ Adverb: **well**   Verb: **drives**

Practice 1

Choose the correct word to finish the sentence. Write the sentences on a separate sheet of paper. The first one is done for you.

1. He spoke (soft, softly) to his dog.

   He spoke softly to his dog.

2. It was a (cold, coldly) December day.

3. Several (brave, bravely) swimmers walked toward the lake.

4. The hard snow crunched (loud, loudly) under their feet.

5. Icicles glistened (bright, brightly) on the branches.

6. The swimmers got ready (silent, silently).

7. (Sudden, Suddenly), one ran toward the lake.

8. She jumped into the (icy, icily) water.

9. Another walked (slow, slowly) to join her.

10. Two swimmers stared (nervous, nervously) at the photographers.

Lesson 5: Using Adverbs to Make Comparisons

Adverbs can be used to compare two or more actions.

☐ When you compare two actions, use an **-er** ending with a few short adverbs. Use **more** or **less** before most adverbs.

He moved **faster** than his brother.

He moved **more quickly** than his brother.

He moved **less quickly** than his brother.

☐ When you compare more than two actions, use an **-est** ending with a few short adverbs. Use **most** or **least** with most adverbs.

He spoke **earliest** of all.

He spoke **most thoughtfully** of all.

He spoke **least thoughtfully** of all.

Practice 1

Rewrite these sentences on a separate sheet of paper. Use the correct form of the adverb. Remember to use the words **more, less, most,** or **least** where necessary. The first one has been done for you.

1. Franny worked (long) than Sal.

   Franny worked longer than Sal.

2. Of all these cut flowers, the orchid will last (long).

3. Dirty snow melts (fast) than clean snow does.

4. A grown dog can bark (fierce) than a puppy can.

5. Of all land mammals, the three-toed sloth moves (slow).

6. Erica sings (high) than anyone in the choir.

7. The winner of the election spoke (convincingly) than the loser.

The forms of the adverb **well** are **well, better,** and **best.**

Use **better** when comparing two.

Use **best** when comparing more than two.

   He writes better than his friend.

   Who writes best of all?

Practice 2

Complete these sentences by using the correct form of the adverb **well.** Write the sentences on a separate sheet of paper. The first one has been done for you.

1. He did _____ on this test than he did on the last one.

    He did better on this test than he did on the last one.

2. Jenny did _____ of all.
3. At night a cat can see _____ than a dog.
4. Jason spoke _____ than Gayle.
5. Who spoke _____ of all the candidates?

Lesson 6: Avoiding Double Negatives

A **negative** is a word or phrase that expresses denial or says "no." **Not** is a negative and it is also an adverb. Pronouns such as **nobody** or **no one** are also negative words.

The words in the box are negative words.

no	not	never	no one	nobody	nothing
nowhere	none	hardly	barely	scarcely

The negative adverb **not** can be joined to a verb. The new word is called a **contraction.** The words in the box below are contractions.

aren't	**are not**	don't	**do not**
won't	**will not**	wouldn't	**will not**

Contractions are often part of a verb phrase.

won't listen	**will not** listen
don't study	**do not** study
should've studied	**should have** studied

A negative word may change the whole meaning of a sentence. Use only one negative word to make a sentence mean **no** or **not**. Avoid double negatives.

No one ever understands how I feel.

My friends **never** understand how I feel.

Hardly anyone understands how I feel.

Bob did **nothing.**

Bob **didn't** do anything.

Bob **never** did anything.

No one did anything.

Challenge

Many people use the word **ain't** in their speech. This contraction is not considered acceptable English and should be avoided. It is different from any other contraction because it can mean several things:

are not, am not, is not, have not, and *has not.*

Change one of these meanings of **ain't** into a contraction. Write a sentence using the contraction.

Practice 1

Rewrite these sentences on a separate sheet of paper. Use only one negative word in each sentence. The first one has been done for you.

1. A centipede doesn't really have no hundred legs.

   A centipede doesn't really have a hundred legs.

2. Bats don't actually carry no bugs.

3. Camels don't hardly store no water in their humps.

4. Nobody didn't believe that story.

5. Birds aren't never frightened by scarecrows.

6. Most gorillas aren't really hardly dangerous.

Lesson 7: Exact Adverbs

Using exact adverbs can make your writing clearer and more interesting.

Read these three sentences. Decide which sentence gives the clearest picture.

Nedra skated.

Nedra skated **well.**

Nedra skated **quickly** and **gracefully.**

The first sentence has no adverbs. It is hard to picture Nedra skating. The adverb **well** has been added to the second sentence. But **well** does not tell much. It is not an exact adverb. Exact adverbs have been added to the last sentence. That sentence gives the clearest picture.

Practice 1

Rewrite these sentences on a separate sheet of paper. Use the most exact adverb. The first one is done for you.

1. That company treats its employees (generously, fairly).

   That company treats its employees generously.

2. The flowers in the vase were arranged (nicely, beautifully).

3. We go to the library (weekly, often).

4. Their dog barked (deafeningly, loudly).

5. The team practices (regularly, daily).

Practice 2

Complete each sentence with an exact adverb of your own. Write the sentences on a separate sheet of paper.

1. The bell rang _____ .

2. That couple dances _____ .

3. She tapped _____ on the door.

4. The committee argued _____ .

5. Jack smiled _____ .

Chapter Review

Chapter Summary

☐ An adverb is a word that tells more about a verb or verb phrase. Adverbs tell how, where, when or how many times something is done. Adverbs also tell more about adjectives and other adverbs.

Adverbs: fast quickly very

☐ Adverbs may be used to make comparisons. Use the **-er** form for a few short adverbs when comparing two actions. Use **more** or **less** before most adverbs.

Comparisons of two actions: faster   more quickly less quickly

☐ Use the **-est** form for a few short adverbs when comparing more than two actions. Use **most** or **least** before most adverbs.

Comparisons of more than two actions: fastest most quickly   least quickly

☐ Use only one negative word in a sentence.

Negative words: no   not   never   no one   nobody

nothing   nowhere   none   hardly   barely   scarcely

Chapter Quiz

A. Use words from the box to complete these sentences on a separate sheet of paper.

adverb	contraction	negative

1. A _____ is a shortened form of a word or group of words.

2. An _____ tells how, where, when, or how many times something is done.

3. A _____ is a word that says "no."

B. Write the adverb from these sentences on a separate sheet of paper. Some sentences have more than one adverb.

1. You should study today.

2. Mayling ran around the track swifly.

3. We shall meet you at the bank later.

4. Someone can bring the bags inside.

5. If you work too quickly, you may make mistakes.

6. Rudy works slowly, but accurately.

C. Rewrite these sentences on a separate sheet of paper. Use the correct form of the adverb to make a comparison.

1. A man runs (slowly) than a charging rhinoceros.

2. The right lung works (hard) than the left one.

3. John Hancock signed the Declaration of Independence (clearly) than anyone else.

4. Among birds, the ostrich runs (fast).

5. Of all the runners, Katherine finishes first (often).

6. Of the seven people who tried out, you danced (well).

Unit Review

A. Rewrite these sentences on a separate sheet of paper. Underline the adjectives once. Underline the adverbs twice.

1. A hulking stranger pushed the door open.

2. The guard looked suspiciously at the frightened boy.

3. The huge crowd moved slowly through the gates.

4. We could hear the blaring noise here.

B. Rewrite these sentences on a separate sheet of paper. Use the correct form of the adverb to make a comparison.

1. Of all the batters in this game, Jerry hit the ball (far).

2. The condor beats its wings (slowly) of all birds.

3. Ms. Wang left (soon) than her sister.

4. Terrance explained the idea (clearly) than I could.

C. Choose the correct word to finish the sentence. Write the sentences on a separate sheet of paper.

1. Most of the reporters stayed inside the (warm, warmly) restaurant.

2. Another stood (brave, bravely) in the snowstorm outside.

3. Two people had been driving (careless, carelessly) and crashed.

4. There was (serious, seriously) damage to both cars.

Unit Six

Phrases

12 Prepositions and Prepositional Phrases

Look at the photograph. Describe how a car might move through this maze. You will probably use words such as to, from, around, behind, into, *and* through. *All of these words are prepositions. In this chapter you will learn about prepositions and how to use them.*

Chapter Learning Objectives

Identify and use prepositions.

Identify and use prepositional phrases.

Use the correct verb form after prepositional phrases.

Words to Know

preposition   a word that shows how a noun or pronoun relates to another word or group of words in a sentence

prepositional phrase   a group of words that begins with a preposition and ends with a noun or pronoun .

Lesson 1: What Is a Preposition?

A **preposition** shows how a noun or pronoun is related to another word or group of words in a sentence.

> The line stretched **around** the corner.
>
> We waited **for** an hour.
>
> The movie was **about** a space flight.

The words in the box below are prepositions.

about	beneath	in	toward
above	beside	into	under
across	besides	like	underneath
after	between	near	until
against	beyond	of	unto
along	but	off	up
amid	by	on	upon
among	concerning	over	with
around	down	past	without
at	during	since	within
before	except	through	
behind	for	throughout	
below	from	to	

Try this for fun!

Suppose you are giving someone directions for getting from your school to your home. You will need to use prepositions. Try to use as many prepositions from the box on page 199 as you can.

Practice 1

Find the prepositions in these sentences. Some sentences have more than one preposition. Write the prepositions on a separate sheet of paper. The first one has been done for you.

1. He came from New York.

   from

2. Bobby Fischer played his first game of chess at the age of five.

3. He learned chess with his sister's help.

4. Within a few years, Fischer was playing in tournaments.

5. Before 1958 was over, he was the youngest grand master in history.

6. He was only 15 at the time.

7. During 1972, he became the first American world champion.

8. He played against Boris Spassky of the Soviet Union.

9. After three years, Fischer stopped defending his championship.

10. Chess is played throughout Europe and America.

Practice 2

Complete these sentences with a preposition of your own. Write the sentences on a separate sheet of paper. The first one has been done for you.

1. Clint found his keys _____ the sofa.

   Clint found his keys underneath the sofa.

2. Will you call me _____ the game?

3. Sid and Marta left the car _____ the field.

4. They had to walk _____ the highway.

5. Several people drove _____ them.

6. The mechanic took them _____ town.

7. The tow truck brought the car _____ the garage.

8. The mechanic worked _____ the car.

9. They waited _____ two hours.

10. The car was not ready _____ the next day.

Lesson 2: What Is a Prepositional Phrase?

Where did you go last weekend? How did you get there? What did you do when you got there? Answer these questions. Use your imagination, and use prepositions in your answers.

A **prepositional phrase** is a group of words that begins with a preposition and ends with a noun or pronoun. There may be other words between the preposition and the noun or pronoun.

> Jo went **to the supermarket.**
>
> The parking lot was filled **with cars.**
>
> She had to park **across the street.**

Practice 1

Find at least one prepositional phrase in each of the sentences below. Write the prepositional phrases on a separate sheet of paper. Draw a line under each preposition. The first one has been done for you.

1. The bus rumbled down the street.

   <u>down</u> the street

2. The Old London Bridge was designed by a priest.

3. The bridge carried people across the Thames River in London.

4. Builders worked on the bridge for thirty years.

5. Wooden houses were built on it.

6. It was the only bridge over the Thames in London.

7. The bridge was an important part of the London scene.

Notice that many prepositions show position: on, across, over, in, under, beside, behind.

Practice 2

Complete these sentences with a prepositional phrase of your own. Write the sentences on a separate sheet of paper. The first one has been done for you.

1. The boxes _____ should be put away.

   The boxes on the table should be put away.

2. Someone _____ can help me.

3. The answer _____ is unusual.

4. Carl left a note _____ .

5. You should call him back _____ .

Lesson 3: Pronouns in Prepositional Phrases

The personal pronouns **me, him, her, it, us, you,** and **them** can be used in prepositional phrases.

Come **with me.**   Is that **for us?**

Give that **to him.**   Keep it **near you.**

The card is **under it.**   Cal was **with them.**

The bus went right **by her.**

Practice 1

Find at least one prepositional phrase in each sentence below. Write the prepositional phrases on a separate sheet of paper. Draw a line under each noun or pronoun in the prepositional phrase. The first one has been done for you.

1. She stood between her friends.

   between <u>her friends</u>

2. A painting of Scott was given to her.

3. A round is a song sung in three parts.

4. The singers each begin at a different time.

5. She came into the room with him.

6. Ken walked by them.

7. Jay did the work for me.

8. Susan sang a song about the West.

Practice 2

Complete these sentences with personal pronouns of your own. Write the sentences on a separate sheet of paper. The first one has been done for you.

1. Claudia went with _____ .

   Claudia went with him.

2. The story is about _____ .

3. Vic drove through _____ .

4. Sandy is somewhere among _____ .

5. Dick arrived after _____ .

6. Leah ran toward _____ .

Lesson 4: Prepositional Phrases in the Subject

The verb or verb phrase in a sentence agrees with the main noun or pronoun in the subject.

Sometimes a prepositional phrase comes after the main noun in the subject. The prepositional phrase is a part of the subject. The verb or verb phrase still agrees with the main noun or pronoun. The verb does not need to agree with the noun or pronoun in the prepositional phrase.

> The **men** on the team **bowl** well.

> The **woman** with the suitcases **is** my aunt.

Practice 1

Rewrite these sentences on a separate sheet of paper. Choose the correct verb form. Draw a line under the main noun or pronoun in the subject. The first one has been done for you.

1. The papers on the table (is, are) mine.

   The <u>papers</u> on the table are mine.

2. The jobs at the park (was, were) listed last.

3. The stars of the play (rehearses, rehearse) daily.

4. The leader of the other groups (agrees, agree) with us.

5. One of the children (cries, cry) constantly.

6. The senators from Ohio (wishes, wish) to speak.

7. The man with all the packages (needs, need) help.

8. The vote of the people (chooses, choose) the president.

Words to the Wise

Birds of a feather flock together.

Write this proverb on a separate sheet of paper. Draw a line under the prepositional phrase. Remember that proverbs are always about people. Explain what this saying means in your own words.

Practice 2

Complete these sentences with a present tense verb form. Write the sentences on a separate sheet of paper. The first one has been done for you.

1. The students from Center High School _____ here often.

   The students from Center High School come here often.

2. The reporters from the television station _____ important questions.

3. The passengers from the plane _____ the terminal.

4. The packages on the table _____ to Ann.

5. Making lunch for my aunts _____ easy.

Lesson 5: Using Prepositions Correctly

Between and **Among**

☐ Use **between** when you refer to two people, things, or groups.
Norm is sitting **between his two sisters.**

☐ Use **among** when you refer to more than two people, things, or groups.
Norm is **among all his relatives.**

Beside and Besides

☐ The preposition **beside** means "next to."
She puts the papers **beside the book.**

☐ The preposition **besides** means "in addition to" or "except."
Besides paper, she bought envelopes, stamps, and pens.

Practice 1

Rewrite these sentences on a separate sheet of paper. Use the correct preposition. The first one has been done for you.

1. Our house is (beside, besides) a lake.

   Our house is beside a lake.

2. (Beside, Besides) Jane, there will be four people.

3. (Among, Between) all the guests, I noticed my cousin.

4. Larry walked (beside, besides) Anita.

5. Nobody (beside, besides) Mark wants to go.

6. You must choose (between, among) the two.

7. Could anyone (beside, besides) Donna do the job?

8. One pine stood (among, between) a forest of elms.

9. The road (among, between) Jamesville and Prescott is lonely.

10. Put the chair (beside, besides) the table.

Chapter Review

Chapter Summary

☐ A preposition shows how a noun or pronoun relates to a word or group of words in the sentence.

Prepositions: for into near under

☐ A prepositional phrase is a group of words that begins with a preposition and ends with a noun or pronoun. There may be other words between the preposition and the noun or pronoun.

Prepositional phrases: with Eric   on that bumpy road

☐ The personal pronouns **me, him, her, it, us, you,** and **them** are used in prepositional phrases.

Prepositional phrase: for them

☐ Use the preposition **between** when you refer to two people, things, or groups.

☐ Use the preposition **among** when you refer to more than two people, things, or groups.

The preposition **beside** means "next to."

The preposition **besides** means "in addition to" or "except."

Chapter Quiz

A. Complete these sentences with the correct word or word group from the box. Write the sentences on a separate sheet of paper.

preposition	prepositional phrase	pronoun

1. A _____ begins with a preposition and ends with a noun or pronoun.

2. A personal _____ can be used in a prepositional phrase.

3. A _____ relates a noun or pronoun to a word or group of words in a sentence.

B. Find at least one prepositional phrase in each sentence below. Write the prepositional phrases on a separate sheet of paper. Draw one line under the preposition. Draw two lines under the noun or pronoun in the prepositional phrase.

1. Teddy Roosevelt once shook hands with 8,513 people in a day.

2. President Taylor did not vote in his own election.

3. President Hoover gave his salary to charity.

4. Martin Van Buren was the first American president born in the United States.

5. Lyndon Johnson served steaks cut in the shape of Texas.

6. Ulysses S. Grant was arrested for speeding on his horse.

C. Read this list of words in the box. On a separate sheet of paper, write only the prepositions.

friendly	about	beside	early	because
an	by	where	long	along

Chapter *13* Other Phrases

How would you describe this scene and the person in it? Simple adjectives might not be enough to do a good job. Using phrases in your description would add variety and more information. This chapter will teach you about different kinds of phrases and how to use them.

Chapter Learning Objectives

Identify and use appositive phrases.

Use appositive phrases to combine sentences.

Identify and use participial phrases.

Use participial phrases to combine sentences.

Identify and use gerund phrases.

Identify and use infinitive phrases.

Words to Know

appositive noun   a noun that follows another noun or pronoun to tell more about it or to rename it

appositive phrase   a phrase containing an appositive noun. An appositive phrase follows a noun or pronoun to tell more about it or to rename it.

gerund   a present participle used as a noun. Gerunds end with **-ing**.

gerund phrase   a phrase that begins with a gerund. Gerund phrases are used as nouns.

infinitive   the word **to** plus the plural form of a verb. Infinitives may be used as nouns.

infinitive phrase   a phrase that begins with an infinitive

participial phrase   a phrase that begins with a present participle or a past participle

Lesson 1: Appositive Nouns and Appositive Phrases

Think about people you know. Use appositive nouns and appositive phrases to describe them. You'll be surprised at how easy this is. Start with a member of your family.

An **appositive noun** follows another noun or pronoun to tell more about it or to rename it.

> The chairperson, **Jeff,** called the meeting to order.

The appositive noun in the sentence above is **Jeff. Jeff** renames **chairperson.**

An **appositive phrase** contains an appositive noun. An appositive phrase is placed next to a noun or pronoun to tell more about it or to rename it.

> Jeff, **the chairperson of the committee,** called the meeting to order.

The chairperson of the committee is the appositive phrase in the sentence above. This phrase renames **Jeff. Chairperson** is the appositive noun in the appositive phrase.

Practice 1

On a separate sheet of paper, write the appositive phrase from each sentence. Draw a line under the appositive noun. The first one is done for you.

1. Baseball, our national game, is also popular in Japan.

    our national <u>game</u>

2. Millions of fans enjoy football, an exciting sport.

3. Boxing, an Olympic sport, consists of fighting with fists.

4. Ping-Pong, a table game, is a competitive sport in China.

5. Field hockey, a game similar to soccer, began in England.

6. The French invented croquet, a lawn game.

7. Jai alai, a game of Spanish origin, is popular in Latin America.

8. A game using a net, volleyball, can be played indoors or outdoors.

9. Chess, a board game for two players, demands thinking.

10. Soccer, a most popular game, is played in more than 100 countries.

Use one or two commas to separate an appositive phrase from the rest of the sentence.

> No one said anything to John, **the secretary**.
> The caller, **a man from George's Garage**, left no message.

Practice 2

Rewrite these sentences on a separate sheet of paper. Use commas to separate the appositive phrases. The first one has been done for you.

1. Andrea a talented artist painted the mural.

   Andrea, a talented artist, painted the mural.

2. Two elephants the most popular animals in the zoo have disappeared.

3. The other movie a long comedy about lawyers was dull.

4. You should have spoken to Ms. Hale the manager of the hotel.

5. Nick found that Jay the best player on the team would be his opponent.

You can use appositive nouns and phrases to combine sentences.

> Helen will be in the first race.
>
> Helen is **the fastest runner on the team**.
>
> Helen, **the fastest runner on the team**, will be in the first race.

Practice 3

Use an appositive noun or phrase to combine each pair of sentences. Write your sentences on a separate sheet of paper. The first one is done for you.

1. James Bond always comes to the rescue.

   Bond is a famous hero.

   James Bond, a famous hero, always comes to the rescue.

2. His expensive car streaks around corners.

   His car is an Aston Martin.

3. Bond often eats his favorite food.

   This food is caviar.

4. James Bond is known under a code name.

   The number 007 is his code name.

5. Miss Moneypenny works for M.

   M is Bond's boss.

Lesson 2: Participial Phrases

How did you get to school today? Did you take a bus or walk? What did you see along the way? Answer these questions by using participial phrases.

A **participial phrase** begins with either a present participle, such as **running**, or a past participle, such as **seated**. A participial phrase gives more information about a noun or pronoun.

> **Running across the field,** the player lost his shoe.
>
> **Seated on the bench,** the coach remained calm.
>
> The fans, **seeing what happened,** laughed.

Practice 1

Copy these sentences on a separate sheet of paper. Draw a line under the participial phrase. The first one is done for you.

1. Understanding the problem, I was able to find an answer.

   Understanding the problem, I was able to find an answer.

2. Arriving late, we walked quietly down the hall.
3. Our friends, having arrived early, were already seated.
4. The old man, arguing calmly, made his point.
5. The choir's voices, singing loudly, filled the hall.
6. Washed with care, this sweater will last a long time.
7. The raisins, baked by the sun, were plump.
8. Crying loudly, the baby demanded attention.
9. The envelope, sealed with wax, was difficult to open.
10. Looking everywhere, we finally found the keys.

You can use a participial phrase to combine sentences.

Read the examples. Notice how a comma or commas are used to separate the participial phrase from the rest of the sentence.

The car **came out of nowhere.**

The car **tore down the street.**

Coming out of nowhere, the car tore down the street.

The car, **coming out of nowhere**, tore down the street.

Practice 2

Change the first sentence in each pair into a participial phrase. Add it to the second sentence. Use a comma or commas to separate the participial phrase from the rest of the sentence. The first one is done for you.

1. I was stalled at the traffic light.

   I waited for the tow truck.

   Stalled at the traffic light, I waited for the tow truck.

2. She arrives early.

   She was also the first to leave.

3. Stanley looked around the corner.

   Stanley noticed the hole in the wall.

4. Hans Christian Anderson began as an actor.

   Hans Christian Anderson became a famous storyteller.

5. George felt ill.

   George returned home.

6. The cat sees a mouse.

   The cat pounces.

Lesson 3: Gerunds and Gerund Phrases

A **gerund** is a present participle, a verb that ends in **-ing**. It is always used as a noun.

Gardening interests many people.

Many people enjoy **gardening.**

Try this for fun!

Make up a list of activities you enjoy, such as swimming, running, dancing, and singing. Notice that your list is made up of gerunds. Now use each of your favorite gerunds in a sentence of your own.

Practice 1

Write the gerunds from these sentences on a separate sheet of paper. The first one is done for you.

1. Reading is important.

   Reading

2. Running can be good exercise.

3. Writing forces you to think.

4. Discoveries can be made by experimenting.

5. You can save time by flying.

6. Sleeping is necessary for good health.

7. You can improve your grades by studying.

8. Some people think cooking is an art.

Practice 2

Copy these sentences on a separate sheet of paper. Add a gerund in each blank.

1. _____ can be helpful.
2. _____ is better than watching television.
3. _____ is fun.
4. _____ is easy.
5. _____ is difficult.

A **gerund phrase** begins with a gerund. The phrase includes one or more other words that add to the meaning of the gerund. A gerund phrase is used as a noun.

> **Growing fruits and vegetables** is my hobby.
>
> My famliy enjoys **eating this fresh produce.**

Practice 3

Write the gerund phrases from these sentences on a separate sheet of paper. The first one is done for you.

1. Shopping for clothes can be difficult.
   Shopping for clothes

2. Finding size four is often impossible.
3. Trying to find a clerk may be hard.
4. He took a long time choosing a sweater.
5. Did you spend all that time paying for your purchase?
6. Remembering names is difficult for Edna.
7. Sallie enjoys choosing presents for her friends.

Practice 4

Copy these sentences on a separate sheet of paper. Add a gerund phrase in each blank.

1. _____ will be fun.
2. _____ can often take a long time.
3. _____ seems easy to learn.
4. _____ has interested many people.
5. _____ is important if you want to succeed.

Lesson 4: Infinitives and Infinitive Phrases

An **infinitive** is made up of the word **to** plus the plural form of the verb.

to think   to read   to work   to speak

Practice 1

Write the infinitives from these sentences on a separate sheet of paper. The first one is done for you.

1. Do you know how to swim?

   to swim

2. Kay learned to dive last Wednesday.

3. It is important to listen.

4. Register to vote here.

5. Hal went to visit his uncle.

An **infinitive phrase** begins with an infinitive. Other words in the phrase tell more about the infinitive. Infinitive phrases can be used as nouns.

> **To lose weight** is Mandy's goal.

> She tries **to limit calories.**

Practice 2

Write the infinitive phrases from these sentences on a separate sheet of paper. The first one is done for you.

1. Randy needed to find the information.

   to find the information

2. Politicians try to persuade people.

3. Grace wanted to succeed in business.

4. It is difficult to know all the answers.

5. A reporter must be able to write quickly.

6. Kathy hurried to catch the train.

7. To understand that lesson is easy.

8. To guess the answer was impossible.

9. Training to become a world-class athlete takes years.

10. She worked to prove her ideas.

Words to the Wise

It is easier to catch flies with honey than with vinegar.

Write this proverb on a separate sheet of paper. Draw a line under the infinitive phrase. Remember that proverbs state a truth or give advice. Explain what this proverb means in your own words.

Hint: Does this proverb just say something about how to catch flies, or is it really about something else?

Chapter Review

Chapter Summary

☐ An appositive noun follows another noun or pronoun to tell more about it or to rename it.

Appositive noun: The new student, **Josh,** answered the question.

☐ An appositive phrase contains an appositive noun.

Appositive phrase: Josh, **the newest student in the class,** answered the question.

☐ A participial phrase begins with a present participle or a past participle.

Participial phrases: Answering the telephone, he got the bad news.

Seated at the desk, she read the entire report.

☐ A gerund is a present participial used as a noun.

Gerund: Smiling is easy.

☐ A gerund phrase is a phrase that begins with a gerund. Gerund phrases are used as nouns.

Gerund phrase: She enjoys **talking with her friends**.

☐ An infinitive consists of the word **to** and the plural form of a verb. An infinitive may be used as a noun.

Infinitive: We went to the zoo **to see** the animals.

☐ An infinitive phrase begins with an infinitive.

Infinitive phrase: It is very important for students **to study carefully.**

Chapter Quiz

A. Complete each sentence with the correct word or word group from the box. Write the sentences on a separate sheet of paper.

appositive noun	appositive phrase	gerund	infinitive
gerund phrase	participial phrase	infinitive phrase	

1. An _____ is made up of the word **to** and the plural form of a verb.

2. An _____ is a noun that tells more about another noun or pronoun.

3. A present or past participial begins a _____ .

4. An _____ begins with an infinitive.

5. An _____ is a phrase that tells more about a noun or pronoun.

6. A _____ is made up of a gerund and other words that tell more about the gerund.

7. A _____ is a word that can be the subject of a sentence.

B. Each sentence contains an appositive phrase, a gerund phrase, a participial phrase, or an infinitive phrase. Write the phrases on a separate sheet of paper. Next to each write the kind of phrase it is.

1. Thinking about the problem made Ann sad.

2. To finish the marathon was his goal.

3. Standing by the door, Jane could see who entered.

4. Mary Yee, the newly-elected president, came in.

5. Seated near an open window, Norm felt chilly.

6. To plan carefully was necessary.

Unit Review

A. Find the prepositional phrases in these sentences. Write the prepositional phrases on a separate sheet of paper. Draw one line under the preposition. Draw two lines under the noun or pronoun in the prepositional phrase.

1. What time should we be at the airport?

2. I shall wait in the lobby.

3. The terminal is on the south side.

4. Park under the terminal.

5. We must carry the suitcases from the car.

6. Keep your ticket near your wallet.

7. You cannot board the plane without a boarding pass.

B. Each sentence contains an appositive phrase, a gerund phrase, a participial phrase, or an infinitive phrase. Write the phrases on a separate sheet of paper. Next to each write the kind of phrase it is.

1. Thinking carefully might help.

2. The house, deserted for years, needed repairs.

3. Roy hoped to win easily.

4. Setting up the telescope took all night.

5. Leaving the building, Jim put on his hat.

6. To get away from the fire quickly was very important.

7. Oscar Peterson, my favorite pianist, gave a concert on Friday.

Unit Seven

Clauses

Chapter 14 Clauses and Conjunctions

A bridge joins *or connects two separate pieces of land. In the same way, a conjunction joins words, word groups, or sentences. In this chapter, you will learn about different kinds of conjunctions and how to use them.*

Chapter Learning Objectives

Identify coordinating conjunctions.

Identify compound sentences.

Use coordinating conjunctions to combine sentences.

Identify subordinating conjunctions.

Identify adverb clauses.

Identify complex sentences.

Use subordinating conjunctions to combine sentences.

Words to Know

adverb clause   a dependent clause that acts as an adverb in a sentence

clause   a group of words that has a subject and predicate and forms part of a sentence. Some clauses can stand alone, others cannot.

complex sentence   a sentence with an independent clause and a dependent clause

compound sentence   a sentence made up of two independent clauses that are joined by a coordinating conjunction

coordinating conjunction   words that are used to join words, groups of words, or sentences: **and, but, or, nor, for, so,** and **yet**

dependent clause   a clause that cannot stand alone as a complete sentence

independent clause   a clause that can stand alone as a complete sentence

simple sentence   a sentence that has one subject and one predicate

subordinating conjunction   a word used to introduce a dependent clause

Lesson 1: What Is a Coordinating Conjunction?

Coordinating conjunctions are used to join words, groups of words, and sentences. The words in the box are coordinating conjunctions.

and	but	or	nor	for	so	yet

Coordinating conjunctions:

Walter **and** Pauline

the black cat **or** the white dog

Jon did not go to the movies, **but** he went to the store.

Practice 1

Copy these sentences on a separate sheet of paper. Draw a line under each coordinating conjunction. The first one has been done for you.

1. Ella or Marie will sing, and Mark will play the piano.

   Ella <u>or</u> Marie will sing, <u>and</u> Mark will play the piano.

2. Margie went, but Al stayed at home.

3. Elizabeth started early; yet she arrived late.

4. His mother and father own a restaurant.

5. Please buy apples or pears.

6. Kim did not come, nor did her sister.

Lesson 2: What Is a Compound Sentence?

In Chapter 1, you learned that every sentence has a subject and a predicate. The sentences in Chapter 1 were simple sentences. Notice how simple sentences can be combined into compound sentences.

A **simple sentence** has one subject and one predicate. The subject, the predicate, or both may be compound.

Simple sentences:

Helen went to the movies.

Helen and Bill went to the movies.

Helen ate dinner and went to the movies.

Helen and Bill ate dinner and went to the movies.

A **compound sentence** is made up of two complete sentences. These complete sentences are called **independent clauses**. A **clause** is a group of words that has a subject and predicate and forms part of a sentence. Some clauses can stand alone as a complete sentence, others cannot. The independent clauses are joined by a coordinating conjunction. So a compound sentence has at least two subjects and two predicates.

Compound sentences:

> Helen ate dinner, and Bill went to the movies.
>
> Manny was the pitcher, and Clara was the shortstop.
>
> Mike scored two runs, but Art did not score any.
>
> We could go to the game, or we could watch it on TV.

The following is not a compound sentence.

> Nora went to the game but did not stay.

The words after **but** are not a complete sentence. They have no subject.

Practice 1

Read the sentences. Some are compound. Some are not. Write only the compound sentences on a separate sheet of paper.

1. One dog ran around the corner, and the other chased him.

2. Gordon read the repair manual, but he could not fix the car.

3. The students wrote papers and read them to the class.

4. Bill is studying auto repair, and his sister is studying carpentry.

5. Jim left his wallet in the car, and I found it.

6. You could show this tomato at the state fair, or you could put it in the salad.

7. I can make dessert or buy it at the store.

8. Sandra called five people, but only one was home.

9. We made the date for eight o'clock.

10. Norma painted the walls, and Steve waxed the floor.

11. The carpet came, but not the curtains.

12. The speaker offered to answer questions, but none were asked.

Lesson 3: Commas in Compound Sentences

Use a comma before the coordinating conjunction in a compound sentence.

Morrie laughed, but Larry was silent.

Practice 1

Copy the sentences on a separate sheet of paper. Place a comma where it is needed. The first one is done for you.

1. Spencer Tracy won an Oscar but the Oscar said, "To Dick Tracy."

   Spencer Tracy won an Oscar, but the Oscar said, "To Dick Tracy."

2. Now barbers just cut hair but they used to do surgery as well.

3. A ball point pen can write on paper or it can write on butter.

4. Cats are small but they have more bones than we do.

5. Some paper contains acid and the acid can destroy it.

Lesson 4: Using Coordinating Conjunctions to Combine Sentences

You can combine two sentences by using a coordinating conjunction and a comma.

You can read the book now.

You can listen to the tape.

You can read the book now, or you can listen to the tape.

Practice 1

Use a coordinating conjunction to combine each pair of sentences into a single sentence. Write your sentences on a separate sheet of paper. The first one has been done for you.

1. The librarian looked up the title.

I found the book on the shelf.

The librarian looked up the title, and I found the book on the shelf.

2. Mickey asked a question.

Mary answered him.

3. Mindy wanted a milk shake.

   Ellen helped her change her mind.

4. George wanted to have dinner.

   The restaurant was closed.

5. You could study a little every night.

   You could study all weekend.

6. Someone dropped by.

   You were not at home.

7. Sam looked the car over.

   Alison filled out the forms.

8. Susan Book really works in a library.

   Dale Dye is a coroner.

9. The witnesses may have been confused.

   They may have been lying.

10. Farmers can grow chickens without feathers.

    These birds catch cold easily.

11. Paul Revere made a midnight ride.

    He billed the Massachusetts government for expenses.

12. I can read a book about pollution.

    I can watch a television program about it.

Challenge

Make up two simple sentences about airplanes. Then combine them into a compound sentence. Remember to use a coordinating conjunction and a comma.

Lesson 5: What Are Subordinating Conjunctions?

A **subordinating conjunction** is a word or group of words that is used to introduce a **dependent clause**. A dependent clause cannot stand alone as a complete sentence.

The words in the box are subordinating conjunctions.

after	because	so that	whenever
although	before	than	where
as	if	though	wherever
as if	in order that	unless	whether
as long as	provided that	until	while
as though	since	when	

Milly lived in this house **until** she moved last fall.

Until she moved last fall, Milly lived in this house.

subordinating conjunction: until

dependent clause: until she moved last fall

Practice 1

Write the subordinating conjunctions from these sentences on a separate sheet of paper. The first one has been done for you.

1. It has been a long time since I saw you.

    since

2. Before you arrived, we finished the work.

3. It was starting to rain when we arrived.

4. We shall come provided that you come, too.

5. She took that course because she wanted a better job.

6. Jerri will wait at the house until you get there.

7. When the sauce boils, remove it from the stove.

8. After it has cooled, put it in the refrigerator.

9. We can do the job whether Paul helps us or not.

10. Whenever you get to the airport, give us a call.

Words to the Wise

When the cat's away, the mice will play.

Write this proverb on a separate sheet of paper. Draw one line under the subordinating conjunction. Draw two lines under the dependent clause. Remember that proverbs are always about people. Explain what this proverb means in your own words.

Practice 2

On a separate sheet of paper, complete these sentences with subordinating conjunctions of your own. The first one is done for you.

1. _____ you sit down, please bring me the paper.

   Before you sit down, please bring me the paper.

2. Tony ate _____ everyone else was served.

3. Sally will baby-sit _____ they return.

4. Rochelle went _____ she thought they were there.

5. Nobody knew how hard Charles worked _____ his partner was ill.

6. Ms. Elyzami will help you _____ she gets here.

7. He will go _____ Donna goes.

8. _____ everyone arrived, we did not know how many people would be here.

9. _____ the meeting, everything was quiet.

10. _____ Kim was at the garage, the house was empty.

Lesson 6: Adverb Clauses in Complex Sentences

A **complex sentence** is a sentence with an independent clause and a dependent clause. A dependent clause that begins with a subordinating conjunction is called an **adverb clause.** An adverb clause is used as an adverb in a sentence. It tells more about a verb, an adjective, or another adverb. An adverb clause answers the question **how, why, where,** or **when.**

Myra arrived before the doors were open.

independent clause: Myra arrived

dependent clause: before the doors were open

subordinating conjunction: before

The dependent clause **before the doors were open** is an **adverb clause** that tells about the verb **arrived.**

Remember: a clause is independent if it can stand alone.

After the doors were open, people poured in.

independent clause: people poured in

dependent clause: after the doors were open

subordinating conjunction: after

The dependent clause **after the doors were open** is an **adverb clause** that tells about the verb **poured**.

Practice 1

Write only the complex sentences on a separate sheet of paper.

A sentence with an adverb clause must also have an independent clause.

1. Everyone laughed when you told the story.
2. Jenny and Lori both turned in a report.
3. Mr. Gee arrived after the concert began.
4. Hasan walked in while the teacher was speaking.
5. She agreed to introduce you if you would sing.
6. No one remembered the man until you described him.
7. Ralph called me and asked a question.
8. Although his job was difficult, Gordon enjoyed it.
9. Benjamin Franklin took a risk when he flew a kite in an electrical storm.
10. Melanie looked as if nothing had happened.

Practice 2

Complete these sentences with adverb clauses of your own. Begin each adverb clause with a subordinating conjunction. Write the sentences on a separate sheet of paper. The first one has been done for you.

Remember: a clause must have a subject and a verb. This is true for adverb clauses as well as all other clauses.

1. _____ , I have been busy.

   Since you have been gone, I have been busy.

2. _____ , Kevin arrived alone.

3. _____ , I had forgotten my speech.

4. _____ , the dog hid in the basement.

5. _____ , stores will be closed.

Lesson 7: Commas in Complex Sentences

Put a comma after the dependent clause if it comes before the independent clause.

Read these sentences. Notice which one has a comma.

He worked hard because he wanted to finish.

independent clause: he worked hard

dependent clause: because he wanted to finish

Because he wanted to finish, he worked hard.

independent clause: he worked hard

dependent clause: because he wanted to finish

Practice 1

Copy these sentences on a separate sheet of paper. Put a comma in each complex sentence that needs one. The first one has been done for you.

1. Because the plane was late we missed our next flight.

   Because the plane was late, we missed our next flight.

2. If you need help ask Ms. Cohen.

3. Until you hear from me please do nothing further.

4. The astronauts grew taller as they traveled in space.

5. Wherever Sam traveled he met interesting people.

6. His health improves when someone visits him.

7. Provided that the weather is good there will be a crowd.

8. Since she moved in Sandra has been busy.

9. As long as Dan was able he helped his father.

Lesson 8: Using Subordinating Conjunctions to Combine Sentences

You can use subordinating conjunctions to combine sentences.

Carlos chose this book.

You liked it.

Carlos chose this book **because** you liked it.

Because you liked it, Carlos chose this book.

Practice 1

Two simple sentences can be combined into a complex sentence. Complex sentences can make your writing or speech clearer and more interesting.

On a separate sheet of paper, combine the sentences in each pair. Use a subordinating conjunction. The first one has been done for you.

1. Karen saw you.

   She went to San Diego.

   Karen saw you when she went to San Diego.

2. Nancy will pick up the twins.

   She goes to the post office.

3. Someone must have been here.

   We arrived.

4. Howard will go to school.

   He wants to build computers.

5. Sol decided to vote for Janice.

   He trusts her.

6. Candace went to the store.

   They were out of groceries.

7. Keith will stay here.

   Mom arrives.

8. Amanda calls us.

   She is in town.

9. Sonny bought the radio.

   It was on sale.

10. Wendy wrote the menu.

    She did not want to.

11. Jay went to the party.

    He was not sure that he would enjoy it.

12. You know the answer.

    Please tell us.

Chapter Review

Chapter Summary

☐ A coordinating conjunction can join words, groups of words, or sentences.

Coordinating conjunctions: and   but   or   nor

for   so   yet

☐ A compound sentence is made up of two sentences or independent clauses. The two sentences are joined by a comma and a coordinating conjunction.

Compound sentence: Jed was in the house, but Meg was in the yard.

☐ A complex sentence is made up of an independent clause and a dependent clause.

Complex sentences: People came although it was cold.

Although it was cold, people came.

Independent clause: people came

Dependent clause: although it was cold

☐ The dependent clause in a complex sentence starts with a subordinating conjunction.

Subordinating conjunction: Ginny visits her uncle **whenever** she is in town.

☐ An adverb clause is a dependent clause that acts as an adverb in a sentence. An adverb clause tells more about a verb.

Adverb clause: He went home **when the class was over.**

☐ A comma is used after the dependent clause if it comes before the independent clause.

Comma usage: If I am late, please start without me.

Chapter Quiz

A. Number a separate sheet of paper from 1 to 6. Match the words in Column A with their definitions in Column B. Write a letter next to each number.

A	B
1. compound sentence	a. a word used to introduce a dependent clause
2. coordinating conjunction	b. a dependent clause that acts as an adverb
3. independent clause	c. a clause that can stand alone as a complete sentence
4. dependent clause	d. a clause that cannot stand alone as a complete sentence
5. complex sentences	e. a sentence that has one subject and one predicate
6. subordinating conjunction	f. a sentence with two independent clauses
7. simple sentence	g. a word used to join words, groups of words, or sentences
8. adverb clause	h. a sentence with an independent clause and a dependent clause

B. Copy these sentences on a separate sheet of paper. Draw one line under the independent clause. Draw two lines under the dependent clause. Circle the subordinating conjunction.

1. If you want to order a shirt, tear out the coupon.

2. Print your name neatly before you do anything else.

3. As we have three colors, please make a choice.

4. Include a check for $9.98 when you mail your order.

5. When we receive your check, we will send you your shirt.

Chapter 15 Adjective Clauses and Noun Clauses

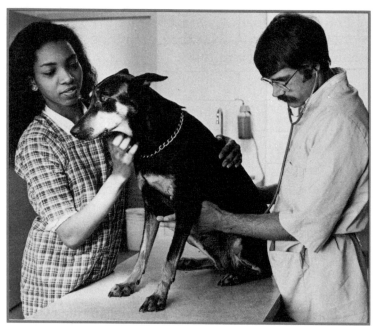

Choose one of the people in the picture. Try to describe exactly what that person looks like and what he or she is doing. Sometimes adjectives and nouns alone are not enough to explain something clearly. In this chapter you will learn about clauses that act as adjectives, adverbs, and nouns in sentences. These clauses can help you express your ideas better.

Chapter Learning Objectives

Identify and use adjective clauses.

Use commas with adjective clauses.

Use adjective clauses to combine sentences.

Identify and use noun clauses.

Words to Know

adjective clause   a dependent clause that acts as an adjective in a sentence

nonrestrictive adjective clause   an adjective clause that is not essential to the meaning of a sentence

noun clause   a dependent clause that is used as a noun in a sentence

restrictive adjective clause an adjective clause that is essential to the meaning of a sentence

Lesson 1: What Is an Adjective Clause?

An **adjective clause** is a dependent clause that acts as an adjective in a sentence. An adjective clause tells more about a noun or a pronoun.

An adjective clause usually begins with a relative pronoun. But it may begin with **where** or **when**.

The words in the box are used to begin adjective clauses.

who	which	that	whom
whose	when	where	

Susan wanted the dog **that was at the pet shop.**

The adjective clause tells more about **dog**.

The woman **whose name I did not know** introduced herself.

Notice that an adjective clause follows the noun or pronoun it tells about.

The adjective clause tells more about **woman**.

Practice 1

Copy these sentences on a separate sheet of paper. Draw a line under the adjective clauses. The first one is done for you.

Remember: a sentence with an adjective clause must also have an independent clause.

1. Tim talked to the woman who left you the message.

   Tim talked to the woman <u>who left you the message.</u>

2. I saw the man whose address you wanted.

3. Marcella took the train that left at 9 o'clock.

4. We could not guess the answers that he would choose.

5. It was a time when we all worked hard.

6. That is a house where many families have lived.

7. We watched the show that you liked so much.

8. We found the keys that you lost on the stairs.

9. Kelly met the man whom you had spoken with last night.

10. You have a teacher who has been at this school for many years.

Practice 2

Complete these sentences with adjective clauses of your own. Begin each adjective clause with **who, which, that, whom, whose, when,** or **where**. Write the sentences on a separate sheet of paper. The first one has been done for you.

1. April 1 is the date _____ .

   April 1 is the date when some people play tricks.

2. Earth is a planet _____ .

3. Here is the man _____ .

4. Those are the people _____ .

5. This is the house _____ .

Try this for fun!

Make up a sentence that tells something about your birthday. Use an adjective clause in your sentence. Write the sentence on a separate sheet of paper.

Lesson 2: Commas with Adjective Clauses

Some adjective clauses are essential to the meaning of a sentence. These adjective clauses are called **restrictive adjective clauses.**

Some adjective clauses are not essential to the meaning of a sentence. These adjective clauses are called **nonrestrictive adjective clauses.** A nonrestrictive adjective clause is set apart from the rest of the sentence by commas.

Scientists **who can use computers** can work faster.

Restrictive adjective clause: **who can use computers**

Jaimie, **who can use a computer,** works here.

Nonrestrictive adjective clause: **who can use a computer**

Practice 1

Rewrite these sentences on a separate sheet of paper. Put a comma before and after each nonrestrictive adjective clause. The first one has been done for you.

1. The vase which is very beautiful is on the table.

    The vase, which is very beautiful, is on the table.

2. The Motown studios which are in Detroit record many top artists.

3. Another celebrity who sings for the Motown label is Stevie Wonder

4. I use my camera which is quite old a good deal.

5. Ted's uncle who was born in Pittsburgh lives with him.

6. That ring which is made of silver belonged to her grandmother.

7. John parked the car which he had just bought in the garage.

8. The book which she enjoyed was an exciting detective story.

9. The carpenter who has been working since noon is Jean's uncle.

10. The weather which had been cold and rainy was expected to improve.

Make up a sentence about something that belongs to you. Use a nonrestrictive adjective clause in your sentence. Write on a separate sheet of paper.

Lesson 3: Using Adjective Clauses to Combine Sentences

You can use adjective clauses to combine sentences.

Remember to begin each adjective clause with a relative pronoun or the word where *or* when.

Harry saw the play.

The play was performed on Wednesday.

Harry saw the play **that was performed on Wednesday.**

The woman left suddenly.

Jenny had talked to the woman.

The woman **whom Jenny had talked to** left suddenly.

Practice 1

Combine the following pairs of sentences on a separate sheet of paper. Make the second sentence an adjective clause in the first sentence. The first one is done for you.

1. The players listened to the coach.

   The coach always gave good advice.

   The players listened to the coach who always gave good advice.

2. In the Northwest lives a creature.

   This creature is known as Bigfoot.

3. Many people have found footprints.

   The footprints supposedly belong to Bigfoot.

4. There is film footage.

   It shows some creature walking upright.

5. Basil read the book.

   The book came from the library.

6. Arnold gave us a shell.

   The shell was from the Florida Keys.

7. The Lakers and the Celtics played a game.

   The game lasted for three hours.

8. Tammy and Mike will take a plane.

   The plane leaves at six o'clock.

9. The plane finally took off.

   The plane had been at the gate for an hour.

10. My uncle showed us the city.

    My uncle has lived in Chicago for ten years.

11. Larry ate lunch in a restaurant.

    The restaurant specialized in pizza.

12. Molly spent the afternoon at a park.

    The park had a beautiful lake.

13. The children played with the toys.

    The toys were made of plastic.

14. Herman was playing a violin.

    The violin was out of tune.

15. Last year there was a storm.

    The storm dumped a foot of snow on the city.

Lesson 4: What Is a Noun Clause?

A **noun clause** is a dependent clause that is used as a noun in a sentence.

A noun clause can begin with one of the words in the box.

how	whatever	which	whose
that	when	who	why
what	where	whoever	whomever

You must remember **what to do in an emergency.**

The noun clause tells what it is that **you must remember**.

Sue thinks **that Jim left the office.**

The noun clause tells what it is that **Sue thinks**.

Practice 1

Rewrite these sentences on a separate sheet of paper. Draw a line under each noun clause. The first one is done for you.

1. I shall never know why we ever went there.

   I shall never know <u>why we ever went there.</u>

2. She found out whose house you had visited.

3. I do not understand why he is always late.

4. The book explains how to do simple repairs.

5. I can't imagine where you lost your glasses.

6. Jeb showed us what was in the basement.

7. Noreen always guesses how a story will end.

8. Tell us what to do when we get there.

9. They asked him what he knew about the accident.

10. Robert told us which bus to take.

Words to the Wise

Whoever profits by the crime is guilty of it.

Write this proverb on a separate sheet of paper. Draw a line under the noun clause. Remember that a proverb states a truth or gives advice. Explain what this proverb means in your own words. Tell whether or not you agree with the proverb's message.

Practice 2

On a separate sheet of paper write only the noun clauses from the following sentences. The first one is done for you.

1. Why she likes him is a mystery.

    Why she likes him is a mystery.

2. Tom is angry about whatever Jim did to him.

3. This stack of coins is what she gave me.

4. Whatever she decides is all right with me.

5. No one knows where she went.

6. Whoever comes late can stand outside.

7. Mary shared whatever she had.

8. Where he will sleep is the problem.

9. How she will manage is anybody's guess.

10. Tell whoever is interested to sign up.

Chapter Review

Chapter Summary

☐ An adjective clause is a dependent clause that acts as an adjective in a sentence. An adjective clause tells more about a noun or pronoun.

> **Adjective clause:** My grandmother has the dishes **that she brought from Europe.**

☐ A nonrestrictive adjective clause is not essential to the meaning of a sentence. Commas set off a nonrestrictive adjective clause from the rest of the sentence.

> **Nonrestrictive adjective clause:** Lisl, **who is a good cook,** served turkey.

☐ A restrictive adjective clause is essential to the meaning of a sentence.

> **Restrictive adjective clause:** Lisl served the turkey **that she had bought the day before.**

☐ A noun clause is a dependent clause that acts as a noun in a sentence.

> **Noun clause: When he will come** is not certain.

Chapter Quiz

A. Number a separate sheet of paper from 1 to 4. Match the words in Column A with their definitions in Column B. Write a letter next to each number.

A	B
1. noun clause	a. a dependent clause that acts as an adjective
2. restrictive adjective clause	b. an adjective clause that is not essential to the meaning of a sentence
3. nonrestrictive adjective clause	c. a dependent clause that is used as a noun
4. adjective clause	d. an adjective clause that is essential to the meaning of a sentence

B. Rewrite the sentences on a separate sheet of paper. Draw one line under each adjective clause. Draw two lines under each noun clause.

1. Nobody knows whose coat that is.

2. Rod bought the stereo that I wanted.

3. Marge is the person who wrote the book.

4. The pin, which was found in the hall, belongs to Kay.

C. On a separate sheet of paper, complete these sentences with noun clauses of your own. Write the sentences on a separate sheet of paper.

1. _____ will get the prize.

2. _____ gave them the wrong information.

3. _____ is something I do not understand.

4. _____ is explained in the film.

Unit Review

A. Copy the sentences below on a separate sheet of paper. Draw one line under each coordinating conjunction and two lines under each subordinating conjunction.

1. Cara came by car and Shirley came by train.

2. Before Mike left I gave him ten dollars.

3. Bill is fast but Melvin is faster.

4. When it snows we'll go skiing.

5. The coach will be here if he can.

6. Unless it rains, the picnic will be held.

7. I'll cook while you clean.

8. We'll play tennis until it gets dark.

B. Combine each clause on the left with a clause on the right to make eight complete sentences. Next to each sentence write **ADJ** if it contains an adjective clause, **ADV** if it contains an adverb clause, and **N** if it contains a noun clause. Write the sentences on a separate sheet of paper.

1. Barry is the player	A. should get in line.
2. He broke the record	B. that burned down.
3. B.J. tells some stories	C. that stood for years.
4. This is the school	D. who hit the home run.
5. Whoever wants lunch	E. how to tell time.
6. Martin gets to school	F. that aren't really true.
7. We won't leave	G. until the show is over.
8. My sister is learning	H. later than his brother.

Appendix

Glossary

Additional Practice Exercises

Reference Guide

Index

Glossary

abbreviation   a shortened form of a word

abstract noun   a noun that names an idea or quality

action verb   a word that expresses physical or mental action

active voice   the form of a verb that indicates the action is performed *by* the subject of a sentence

adjective   a word that describes a noun or a pronoun. Adjectives usually tell what kind, which one, or how many.

adjective clause   a dependent clause that acts as an adjective in a sentence

adverb   a word that tells more about a verb or verb phrase. An adverb tells how, where, when, or how many times something is done. Adverbs also modify adjectives or other adverbs.

adverb clause   a dependent clause that acts as an adverb in a sentence

antecedent   the noun or nouns that the pronoun replaces

apostrophe   ʼ   a punctuation mark that is used to show that something belongs to a person or thing; it is also used in a contraction

appositive noun   a noun that follows another noun or pronoun to tell more about it or to rename it

appositive phrase   a phrase containing an appositive noun. An appositive phrase follows a noun or pronoun to tell more about it or to rename it.

articles   the adjectives *a, an,* and *the*

clause   a group of words that has a subject and predicate and forms part of a sentence. Some clauses can stand alone, others cannot.

colon   :   a punctuation mark that is used to introduce a series of items

comma   ,   a punctuation mark that indicates a short pause between words or groups of words

common noun   a word that names any person, place, thing, event, or idea

complex sentence   a sentence with an independent clause and a dependent clause

compound sentence   a sentence made up of two independent clauses that are joined by a coordinating conjunction

concrete noun   a noun that names something that can be seen, heard, touched, smelled, or tasted

contraction   a shortened form of a word or group of words, in which an apostrophe takes the place of the missing letter or letters

coordinating conjunction   words that are used to join words, groups of words, or sentences: *and, but, or, nor, for,* and *yet*

declarative sentence   a sentence that tells what someone or something is or does

demonstrative pronoun   a pronoun that points out one or more persons, places, or things

dependent clause   a clause that cannot stand alone as a complete sentence

direct object   a noun or pronoun that receives the action of a verb

exclamatory sentence   a sentence that shows strong feeling

future tense   a verb form that shows action that will occur in the future. It is formed by using the words *will* or *shall* with a plural verb form.

gerund   a present participle used as a noun. Gerunds end with *-ing*.

gerund phrase   a phrase that begins with a gerund. Gerund phrases are used as nouns.

helping verb   the verb in a verb phrase that helps the main verb tell what happens or what is

hyphen   -   a punctuation mark that is used between parts of compound numbers, fractions, and certain compound words

imperative sentence   a sentence that gives a command or makes a request

indefinite pronoun   a pronoun that does not replace a particular noun

independent clause   a clause that can stand alone as a complete sentence

indirect object   a noun or pronoun to whom or for whom an action is done

infinitive   the word *to* plus the plural form of a verb. Infinitives may be used as nouns.

infinitive phrase   a phrase that begins with an infinitive

interjection   a word that expresses emotion and that is followed by an exclamation point or comma

interrogative pronoun   a pronoun that is used to ask a question

interrogative sentence   a sentence that asks a question

linking verb   a word that expresses what is or what seems to be

main verb   the verb in a verb phrase that tells what happens or what is

negative   a word or phrase that expresses denial or says "no," such as *not*

nonrestrictive adjective clause   an adjective clause that is not essential to the meaning of a sentence

noun   a word that names a person, place, thing, event, or idea

noun clause   a dependent clause that is used as a noun in a sentence

object complement   a noun or adjective that follows the direct object and refers back to it

participial phrase   a phrase that begins with a present participle or a past participle

passive voice   the form of a verb that indicates the action is performed *upon* the subject of a sentence

past participle   a form of a verb usually made by adding *d, ed, n,* or *en* to the plural verb form

past tense   a verb form that shows action or being in the past

personal pronoun   a word that takes the place of a noun, a group of nouns, or a group of words that includes a noun

plural noun   a noun that names more than one person, place, thing, event, or idea

possessive noun   a noun that shows ownership or relationship

possessive pronoun   a pronoun that shows ownership or relationship

predicate   the part of the sentence that tells what the subject does or is

predicate nominative   a noun or pronoun that follows a linking verb or verb phrase. The predicate nominative renames the subject noun or pronoun.

preposition   a word that shows how a noun or pronoun relates to another word or group of words in a sentence

prepositional phrase   a group of words that begins with a preposition and ends with a noun or pronoun

present participle   a form of a verb usually made by adding *ing* to the plural verb form

present tense   a verb form that shows action or being in the present time

proper adjective   an adjective formed from a proper noun. Proper adjectives refer to the names of particular persons, places, things, events, and ideas.

proper noun   a word that names a particular person, place, thing, event, or idea

quotation marks   " "   punctuation marks that are used to show the beginning and end of someone's exact words

reflexive pronoun   a pronoun that refers back to a noun or pronoun already named

relative pronoun   a pronoun that connects a noun or pronoun with a group of words that tells more about it

restrictive adjective clause   an adjective clause that is essential to the meaning of a sentence

semicolon   ;   a punctuation mark that is used to show a stronger break in thought than that shown by a comma but less than that shown by a period

sentence   a group of words that expresses a complete thought

simple predicate   the verb or verb phrase of a sentence

simple sentence   a sentence that has one subject and one predicate

simple subject   the subject noun or pronoun of a sentence

singular noun   a noun that names one person, place, thing, event, or idea

specific noun   a noun that gives more information about a person, place, or thing

subject   the part of the sentence that tells who or what the sentence is about

subordinating conjunction   a word used to introduce a dependent clause

tense   the time of the action or being expressed by a verb

verb   a word that expresses action or being

verb phrase   a phrase made up of one or more helping verbs and a main verb

Additional Practice: Chapter 1

A. Copy these sentences on a separate sheet of paper. Draw one line under the subject and two lines under the predicate. If the subject is understood, write **you**.

1. This animal looks strange.

2. Look at that lizard.

3. It is called a chameleon.

4. Have you seen one before?

5. When will the chameleon change its color?

B. Copy these sentences on a separate sheet of paper. Put in needed capital letters, periods, question marks, and exclamation points.

1. octopus is a popular food in many parts of the world

2. who plays shortstop on the *Peanuts* baseball team

3. butterflies can get drunk on certain kinds of flowers

4. fleas and dogs are often found together

C. Complete these sentences on a separate sheet of paper. Add a subject or a predicate to each.

1. The noise _____ .

2. The shock _____ .

3. _____ leaped over the fence.

4. No one _____ .

Additional Practice: Chapter 2

A. Copy these sentences on a separate sheet of paper. Put a period, question mark, or exclamation point at the end of each sentence.

1. What could Thomas Adams make from tree sap

2. Perhaps he could make rubber

3. Could he make glue

4. All he could make was chewing gum

5. Great idea

B. Copy these sentences on a separate sheet of paper. Put commas where they are needed.

1. They ate chicken carrots and broccoli.

2. Please buy milk eggs lettuce tomatoes and corn.

3. No she did not call.

4. He lives in New City South Dakota.

5. Donna bought her car on March 21 1995.

C. Copy these sentences on a separate sheet of paper. Put quotation marks, commas, periods, and question marks where they are needed.

1. The bigger box is yours said Sue

2. Who sent me this asked Mark

3. I have no idea answered Sue who sent it

4. It is certainly a mystery Mark said

5. Isn't there a return address asked Sue

Additional Practice: Chapter 3

A. Write the nouns from each sentence on a separate sheet of paper. Write **C** next to each common noun and **P** next to each proper noun.

1. My cousins live in Brazil.

2. The plane will land in Los Angeles.

3. That book is about Japan.

4. Bill Cosby is a very funny actor.

5. The Celtics play basketball in Boston.

B. Complete these sentences on a separate sheet of paper. Add a common noun and a proper noun to each sentence.

1. My _____ lives in the city of _____ .

2. Last _____ we visited _____ .

3. _____ plays the _____ in the orchestra.

4. Did _____ get a _____ at Union Bank?

5. Every winter we go to_____ to visit my _____ .

C. Copy these sentences on a separate sheet of paper. Draw one line under each common noun and two lines under each proper noun.

1. We had a big dinner on Thanksgiving.

2. Mr. Ramirez will visit our class.

3. Nancy Chen works in the store on Friday.

4. The assistant coach is Howard Goldblume.

5. Will Susan Shultz join the team?

Additional Practice: Chapter 4

A. Copy these sentences on a separate sheet of paper. Add 's or ' to each underlined noun to make it possessive.

1. Did you change the <u>dog</u> water.

2. Javier found a <u>girl</u> purse in the store.

3. Have you seen <u>Midori</u> paintings?

4. Nobody has heard the <u>boys</u> story.

5. Amy read the <u>company</u> answer to her letter.

B. On a separate sheet of paper, write the plural form of each noun.

1. dish   5. ox

2. man   6. sheep

3. apple   7. ditch

4. mouse   8. house

C. Write the more specific noun from each sentence on a separate sheet of paper.

1. We took a trip around the (area, city).

2. Elise has studied (ballet, dance).

3. Mioko caught the (fish, flounder).

4. Most (people, teachers) enjoy working with their students.

5. Our (trip, vacation) lasted one week.

6. Nan and I had (chicken, meat) for lunch.

7. We went to the (store, supermarket) after work.

Additional Practice: Chapter 5

A. Write only the pronouns from each sentence on a separate sheet of paper. Write **P** next to each personal pronoun. Write **Pos** next to each possessive pronoun. Write **I** next to each indefinite pronoun.

1. He spoke to everyone.

2. Please give it to him.

3. She noticed something was missing.

4. Sybill spoke about her family.

5. He decided someone had been in the room.

B. Rewrite these sentences on a separate sheet of paper. Change each underlined noun or word group to a pronoun.

1. Please pass the salt to Doris.

2. John and Mia took the package to George.

3. Carmen gave the tickets to Jenny.

4. Rupert and I borrowed Bill's car.

5. Donna works in Tim's office.

C. Complete these sentences on a separate sheet of paper. Add an indefinite pronoun to each.

1. Gloria looked to see if there was _____ to eat.

2. _____ had read the entire chapter.

3. Mark had told _____ about the plan.

4. Manny tried to warn _____ .

5. _____ was listening to Douglas's story.

Additional Practice: Chapter 6

A. Write the pronouns from each sentence on a separate sheet of paper. Write **D** next to each demonstrative pronoun. Write **R** next to each relative pronoun. Write **I** next to each interrogative pronoun.

1. Who took notes on the biology lecture?

2. What is the correct answer?

3. These are the books that Helen ordered.

4. What did you plan to do?

B. Complete these sentences on a separate sheet of paper. Add a demonstrative pronoun or an interrogative pronoun to each sentence.

1. _____ sells the best fruit in town?

2. _____ are the best.

3. From _____ did it come?

4. _____ one is better than that one.

C. Complete these sentences on a separate sheet of paper. Add a relative pronoun to each sentence.

1. The man _____ was driving the red truck is my friend.

2. The envelope _____ contained the letter disappeared.

3. The woman _____ made the discovery seemed nervous.

4. The book _____ fell on the floor is my favorite novel.

Additional Practice: Chapter 7

A. Write the verbs from each sentence on a separate sheet of paper. Write **A** next to each action verb. Write **L** next to each linking verb.

1. Norman became worried.

2. The milk was sour.

3. Ms. Hong enjoyed that book.

4. Everyone played basketball after the picnic.

5. The newcomer seemed pleasant.

B. Copy these sentences on a separate sheet of paper. Use the correct verb form.

1. I (remembers, remember) my trip to Chicago.

2. Chicago (is, are) the largest city in Illinois.

3. Some people (calls, call) Chicago "the windy city."

4. We (believes, believe) that it deserves the name.

5. Few (want, wants) the dessert.

C. Copy these sentences on a separate sheet of paper. Use the correct past tense verb form.

1. The lake (froze, freezed) last night.

2. The old man (were, was) asleep.

3. Dan (chose, chosed) the smallest package.

4. The children (burst, bursted) into the room.

5. Harold (tore, teared) the paper to shreds.

Additional Practice: Chapter 8

A. Copy these sentences on a separate sheet of paper. Draw one line under the helping verb and two lines under the main verb.

1. Thomasina was waiting for the bus.

2. Derrick is calling from the dentist's office.

3. Michael had spoken to this group often.

4. Charlene can explain the work to you.

5. He did play a good game yesterday.

B. Complete these sentences on a separate sheet of paper. Add a helping verb to each sentence.

1. The dogs _____ sleeping in the patio.

2. Roberto _____ driven all night.

3. Our friends _____ play on the other teams.

4. The sweater _____ shrunk in the washing machine.

5. The party _____ begin at eight.

C. Copy only the sentences with passive verb phrases on a separate sheet of paper.

1. The party was given by Grace's mother.

2. The evening was enjoyed by everyone.

3. Jeff was singing when I arrived.

4. The song was written by his brother.

5. The guests thanked the hosts.

Additional Practice: Chapter 9

A. Write the simple subject and simple predicate from each sentence on a separate sheet of paper.

1. The last dodo bird died in 1681.

2. Chickens eat faster in groups than alone.

3. No dog can hear the lowest note on a piano.

4. A hog has better eyesight than a human being.

5. Young seals must be taught to swim.

B. Write the indirect object and the direct object from each sentence on a separate sheet of paper. After the indirect objects, write **IO**. After the direct objects, write **DO**.

1. Tom may have given you some good advice.

2. Her friends bought Tina a going-away present.

3. These results will teach some people a lesson.

4. The artist handed the collector several sketches.

5. The architect showed the builder the blueprints.

C. Write the predicate nominative from each sentence on a separate sheet of paper.

1. Steve McPeak has become a famous daredevil.

2. His tightrope walk was a fantastic stunt.

3. Yosemite Valley is an amazing place.

4. The man we spoke to was a park ranger.

5. He said he was a mountain climber.

Additional Practice: Chapter 10

A. Write the adjectives from each sentence on a separate sheet of paper. Do not write the articles, **a, an**, or **the**.

1. The ending of *Romeo and Juliet* is sad.

2. Alex Haley wrote the popular novel, *Roots*.

3. Harriet Beecher Stowe was an American writer.

4. *Uncle Tom's Cabin* was famous.

5. The prettiest flowers are in the vase.

B. Copy each of these sentences on a separate sheet of paper. Use the correct form of the adjective.

1. A whale is (large) than an elephant.

2. Tina is a (big) dog than Amos.

3. Tina is the (big) dog in obedience class.

4. This is a (tall) office building than that one.

5. April can be the (wet) month of the year.

C. Complete each of these sentences on a separate sheet of paper with an adjective of your own.

1. The _____ quilt feels very soft.

2. Where is the _____ house in town?

3. That is the _____ song you have written.

4. Bill is the _____ man on the team.

5. Maureen likes to go to the beach on _____ days.

Additional Practice: Chapter 11

A. Write the adverbs from each sentence on a separate sheet of paper.

1. Later, we shall meet you at the bank.

2. You should study today.

3. Someone brought the bags inside.

4. Take this test carefully.

5. He spoke rapidly to his friend.

B. Copy each of these sentences on a separate sheet of paper. Use the correct form of the adverb.

1. I slept (late) of all.

2. Evelyn sang (loud) than anyone.

3. Jim is the (fast) runner on the team.

4. Sidney answered (slowly) than Roger.

5. Dr. Irwin will arrive (soon) than Dr. Jones.

C. Copy these sentences on a separate sheet of paper. Use the correct word, either an adjective or adverb, to complete each sentence.

1. He sat (comfortable, comfortably) in the chair.

2. Maurice looked (sad, sadly) at his wrecked car.

3. Marie cooks (good, well).

4. Sandy was very (excited, excitedly).

5. She worked very (careful, carefully).

Additional Practice: Chapter 12

A. Write the prepositional phrase from each sentence on a separate sheet of paper. Underline the preposition.

1. Alice saw a white rabbit with pink eyes.

2. The rabbit was talking to himself.

3. The watch in the rabbit's paw surprised Alice.

4. She followed the rabbit across a field.

5. The rabbit led Alice into Wonderland.

B. Complete each of these sentences with a prepositional phrase of your own. Write your sentences on a separate sheet of paper.

1. The island _____ is called Catalina.

2. Our cousin _____ arrives Tuesday.

3. The man _____ visited the court.

4. The dictionary _____ is the newest.

5. The answer _____ is easy.

C. Use each of these prepositional phrases in a sentence of your own. Write your sentences on a separate sheet of paper.

1. along the road

2. of the answers

3. between the others

4. at the party

5. behind the door

Additional Practice: Chapter 13

A. Write the appositive or participial phrase in each sentence on a separate sheet of paper. If the phrase is appositive, write **A** next to it. If it is participial, write **P**.

1. Victoria, the English Queen, was known for her strict rules.

2. Mel, one of my brother's friends, came by yesterday.

3. Looking at the audience, Jane began her speech.

4. Jesse Owens, a great athlete, won four Olympic medals.

B. Write the infinitive or gerund phrase in each sentence on a separate sheet of paper. If the phrase is a gerund phrase, write **G** next to it. If it is an infinitive phrase, write **I**.

1. To solve the mystery was Sherlock Holmes' goal.

2. Finding clues was vital.

3. Deciding what the clues meant was even more important.

4. Dr. Watson attempted to help Holmes.

C. Use each of these gerund phrases in a sentence of your own. Write your sentences on a separate sheet of paper.

1. sitting on the couch

2. laughing at his joke

3. eating a slice of apple pie

4. running away

Additional Practice: Chapter 14

A. Copy only the compound sentences on a separate sheet of paper. Draw a line under the coordinating conjunctions.

1. Lassie was the star of the show, but Pokey also had fans.

2. Superman had a horse named Krypto and a dog named Comet.

3. A boy released a helium-filled balloon in New York, and it floated to Australia.

B. Copy these complex sentences on a separate sheet of paper. Draw one line under the main clause. Draw two lines under the dependent clause. Circle the subordinating conjunction.

1. The three American astronauts grew taller while they traveled in space.

2. Before Standard Time was established, the United States had more than 80 time zones.

3. If you want to wait, the dentist can see you in twenty minutes.

C. Copy these sentences on a separate sheet of paper. Use commas wherever necessary.

1. Unless you decide to join us we shall not go.

2. When World War I began a British soldier became separated from his group.

3. Because she wanted to help him a French woman hid him in her closet.

4. Until the war was over he stayed there.

Additional Practice: Chapter 15

A. Copy these sentences on a separate sheet of paper. Draw one line under each adjective clause. Draw two lines under each word that begins an adjective clause.

1. John is a person who works very hard.

2. Hermina found a table that no one had noticed.

3. It was a time when everyone seemed excited.

4. We found a store that carried all the items.

B. Copy these sentences on a separate sheet of paper. Draw one line under each noun clause. Draw two lines under each word that begins a noun clause.

1. That the cave existed had been known for years.

2. No one knew why it had never been explored.

3. Who would volunteer had to be decided.

4. Reporters went along to cover whatever took place.

C. Use each of these adjective clauses in a sentence of your own. Write your sentences on a separate sheet of paper.

1. who left this package

2. whose coat this is

3. that listed all the classes

4. who picked up the briefcase

5. that floated down the river

Reference Guide

Chapter 1: Parts of the Sentence

1. What Is a Sentence?

A sentence is a group of words that expresses a complete thought. Every sentence must have a subject and a predicate. Every sentence begins with a capital letter and ends with a punctuation mark.

That leopard has already killed 400 people.

Is it still hungry?

Be careful!

2. Kinds of Sentences

There are four different kinds of sentences. A declarative sentence makes a statement. A declarative sentence ends with a period.

A volcano in the Canary Islands is for sale.

An interrogative sentence asks a question. An interrogative sentence ends with a question mark.

Who would want to buy a volcano?

An imperative sentence gives a command. An imperative sentence ends with a period or an exclamation point.

Show me the list of buyers.

Give that to me right now!

An exclamatory sentence expresses excitement. An exclamatory sentence ends with an exclamation point.

They must be crazy!

3. Subjects and Predicates in Declarative Sentences

Every sentence has two main parts, the subject and the predicate. The subject tells what the sentence is about. The predicate tells something about the subject. In most declarative sentences, the subject is the first part.

A famous sea captain was often sick.

He suffered from seasickness.

In some declarative sentences, the subject is the second part. The predicate is the first part.

Back and forth rolled **the captain's ship.**

4. Subjects and Predicates in Interrogative Sentences

Every interrogative sentence has a subject and a predicate. In some interrogative sentences the subject is the first part. The predicate is the second part.

Who solved the mystery?

Which clue was most important?

In most interrogative sentences, part of the predicate comes before the subject. To find the subject and predicate, rearrange the words of the interrogative sentence. Use those words to make a declarative sentence. (The declarative sentence will not always sound natural, but it will help you.) The subject and predicate of both sentences are the same.

Why did **the butler** lie about it?

The butler did lie about it why.

5. Subjects and Predicates in Imperative Sentences

Only the predicate of an imperative sentence is spoken or written. The subject of the sentence is understood. The subject is always **you.**

(You) Try an underhand serve.

(You) Please show me how to do it.

6. Capital Letters and End Punctuation in Sentences

Every sentence begins with a capital letter.

The train went into the tunnel.

Use a period at the end of a declarative sentence.

A hockey player must be able to skate backward quickly.

Use a question mark at the end of an interrogative sentence.

Who is the goalie for their team?

Use a period or an exclamation point at the end of an imperative sentence.

Keep your eye on the puck.

Pass that puck now!

Use an exclamation point at the end of an exclamatory sentence.

That was a terrific block!

Chapter 2: Punctuation

1. Using Commas to Avoid Confusion in a Sentence

Use a comma to make the meaning of a sentence clearer.

The traffic was slowing down, he noticed.

Early in the morning, trucks made deliveries.

2. Using Commas in a Series

Three or more words or groups of words used in the same way in a sentence form a series. Use commas to separate the words or word groups in a series.

Jamie, Mitch, Kim, and Pablo entered the contest.

Each contestant swam one mile, bicycled two miles, and ran five miles.

3. Using Commas to Set Off Words in a Sentence

Sometimes a sentence begins with an introductory word or group of words. Use a comma to separate these words from the rest of the sentence.

In the old dresser, Penny found the diamonds.

Sometimes words interrupt a sentence. Use commas before and after such words.

That is, I think, the best idea of all.

Use a comma after a noun of address at the beginning of a sentence.

Gloria, that was a terrific pitch!

Use a comma before a noun of address at the end of a sentence.

> That was a terrific pitch, Gloria.

If a noun of address comes in the middle of a sentence, use commas before and after the noun of address.

> That, Gloria, was a terrific pitch.

---

4. Using Punctuation Correctly with Direct Quotations

A direct quotation tells the exact words the person said. Use quotation marks at the beginning and end of each part of a direct quotation.

> "Look," cried Tom, "that cat is smiling!"

> "Of course," said Tina, "it's a Cheshire cat."

Usually use a comma to separate the words of a direct quotation from the words that tell who is speaking.

> Jay asked, "Who won the game last night?"

> "The Cubs won it," said Linda, "in 14 innings."

If a direct quotation is at the end of the sentence, use a period, question mark, or exclamation point.

> Linda said, "The Cubs won last night's game."

> Jay asked, "Did you see the game?"

> Linda replied, "Yes. It was great!"

Sometimes the direct quotation comes before the name of the speaker. If the quotation is a statement or command, use a comma at the end of it. If the quotation is a question, use a question mark. If the quotation is an exclamation, use an exclamation point.

> "The Cubs won last night's game," said Linda.

> "Was it an exciting game?" asked Mel.

"Tell us about the game," said Jay.

"It was great!" yelled Linda.

Begin the first word in a direct quotation with a capital letter.

Dr. Pavlik said, "There are no teeth in the denture law."

If the words that tell who is speaking come in the middle of a sentence, do not begin the second part of the quotation with a capital letter.

"There are no teeth," said Dr. Pavlik, "in the denture law."

5. Using Commas in Dates and in Place Names

Use a comma between the number of the day and the number of the year in a date.

Hank Aaron hit his record-breaking home run on April 8, 1974.

If a date does not come at the end of a sentence, put another comma after the end of the year.

April 8, 1974, was an exciting day for Hank Aaron's fans.

Do not use a comma in a date that has only the name of the month and the number of the year.

Aaron hit his final home run in July 1976.

Use a comma between the name of a city or town and the name of a state or country.

The world's largest chocolate factory is in Hershey, Pennsylvania.

If the two names do not come at the end of a sentence, put another comma after the name of the state or country.

Hershey, Pennsylvania, is the home of the world's largest chocolate factory.

6. Using Commas or Exclamation Points with Interjections

An interjection is a word or group of words that expresses feeling.

Use a comma after an interjection at the beginning of a sentence.

Well, we should probably think about it.

Use an exclamation point after an interjection that expresses excitement.

Wow! That's the best idea of all.

7. Using Colons, Semicolons, and Hyphens

Use a colon to introduce a list of items.

This is what she will do: read a book, cook dinner, and go to the movies.

Use a colon after the greeting in a business letter.

Dear Mrs. Huan: Dear Dr. Simon: Dear Sir:

When you use numerals to write time, use a colon between the hour and the minutes.

5:45 P.M.   9:00 A.M.   12:17 P.M.

Use a semicolon to show a break in thought in a sentence.

Jill waited two hours at the station; the train was late.

Use a hyphen in a compound number from twenty-one to ninety-nine.

thirty-seven   fifty-eight   seventy-three

Use a hyphen in a fraction.

one-quarter   two-thirds   seven-eighths

Use a hyphen in certain compound words.

mother-in-law   speed-reading

Chapter 3: Common and Proper Nouns

1. What Are Nouns?

A noun is a word that names a person, place, thing, event, or idea.

> The **students** watching the **race** from the **stadium** waved their **flags** with **enthusiasm**.

2. Common and Proper Nouns

A common noun is the name of any person, place, thing, event, or idea.

> The man stopped in the town and ate a hamburger.

A proper noun is the name of a particular person, place, thing, event, or idea. Each important word in a proper noun begins with a capital letter.

> **Max** stopped in **Junctionville** and ate a **Big Mac**.

3. Using Proper Nouns Correctly

Almost always begin each part of a person's name with a capital letter.

> Toby Ohara   Rose Delaney   Sue Ellen Macmillan

Some names have more than one capital letter. Other names have parts that are not capitalized.

> Tim O'Hara   Tony de la Cruz   Jean McIntyre

Use capital letters to write an initial that is part of a person's name.

> B. J. Gallardo   J. Kelly Hunt   John F. Kennedy

Begin the title before a person's name with a capital letter.

> Mr. Sam Yee   Dr. Watson   Mayor Jan Hill

Do not use a capital letter if this kind of word is not used before a person's name.

> Did you call the doctor?

> Who will be the city's next mayor?

A word such as grandma or uncle may be used as a person's name or part of a person's name. Begin this kind of word with a capital letter.

> Only Dad and Aunt Ellie understand it.

Usually, if a possessive pronoun comes before a word like grandma or uncle, do not begin that word with a capital letter.

> Only my dad and my aunt understand it.

Begin the name of a day with a capital letter.

> Most people don't have to work on Sunday.

Begin the name of a month with a capital letter.

> At the equator the hottest months are March and September.

Begin each important word in the name of a holiday with a capital letter. Words such as **the** and **of** do not begin with capital letters.

> They have a picnic on the Fourth of July.

> Will you come to dinner on Thanksgiving?

Begin each important word in the name of a street or highway with a capital letter.

> Why is Lombard Street known as the most crooked street in the world?

Begin each word in the name of a city or town with a capital letter.

> In 1957, the Dodgers moved from Brooklyn to Los Angeles.

Begin each word in the name of a state, country, or continent with a capital letter.

> The story was set in New Mexico.
>
> They shot the film in Mexico.
>
> There are high mountains in Antarctica.

Begin each word in the name of a mountain, river, lake, or ocean with a capital letter.

> Amelia Earhart's plane was lost over the Pacific Ocean.

Chapter 4: Other Nouns

1. Singular and Plural Nouns

Almost every noun has two forms. The singular form names one person, place, thing, event, or idea.

> Only one worker in that factory can name the secret ingredient.

The plural form names more than one person, place, thing, event, or idea.

> Several workers in those factories can name the secret ingredients.

2. Spelling Plural Nouns Correctly

Most nouns add *s* to make the plural form.

> cartoon — cartoons   joke — jokes

Nouns that end in **-s, -sh, -ch, -x** or **-z** add **es.**

> bus — buses   witch — witches
>
> wish — wishes   fox — foxes

Nouns that end in a consonant and -**y** change the **y** to **i** and add **es**.

spy — spies   discovery — discoveries

Nouns that end in -**f** usually change the **f** to **v** and add **es**.

half — halves   loaf — loaves

Nouns that end in -**fe** usually change the **f** to **v** and **s**.

wife — wives   knife — knives

Some exceptions:

roof — roofs   chief — chiefs

safe — safes

If the singular form ends in -**o**, add **s** to some words and **es** to others.

piano — pianos   studio — studios

hero — heroes   tomato — tomatoes

Some nouns change some of their letters to make the plural form.

child — children   mouse — mice

woman — women   goose — geese

A few nouns have the same singular and plural form.

sheep — sheep   deer — deer

3. Possessive Nouns

Possessive nouns show ownership or relationship. Usually singular possessive nouns are made by adding an apostrophe and **s**.

The cage belongs to one bird. It is the bird's cage.

The possessive form of a plural noun that ends in -**s** is made by adding only an apostrophe.

The cage belongs to both birds. It is the birds' cage.

4. Concrete and Abstract Nouns

A concrete noun names something you can see, hear, touch, smell, or taste.

An abstract noun names an idea or a quality.

> concrete nouns: chair, horse
>
> abstract nouns: honesty, courage

5. Specific Nouns

A specific noun gives more information about a person, place, or thing than a nonspecific noun.

> nonspecific nouns: music, color
>
> specific nouns: symphony, blue

Chapter 5: Pronouns and Antecedents

1. Personal Pronouns

A personal pronoun takes the place of a noun, a group of nouns, or a group of words that includes a noun.

> Robert lost the book. **He** lost **it.**

Each personal pronoun has two forms. These forms are used in different ways in sentences.

I	you	he	she	it	we	you	they
me	you	him	her	it	us	you	them

> **He** saw through a wall and read the wrong eye chart.
>
> The army would not accept **him**.

The noun or group of nouns that a pronoun replaces is called its antecedent.

> **Roy Rogers** became famous in the movies. He had an almost equally famous horse, Trigger.

> **Roy Rogers** and **Dale Evans** often worked together. They made dozens of movies.

2. Reflexive Pronouns

A reflexive pronoun refers back to a noun or pronoun already named. Reflexive pronouns end with **-self** or **-selves: myself, yourself, himself, herself, itself, ourselves, yourselves, themselves**.

> The witness had been talking to **himself.**

> You should have bought **yourself** a ticket.

3. Possessive Pronouns

Possessive pronouns show ownership or relationship.

These possessive pronouns are used before nouns: **my, your, his, her, its, our, their**.

> Why are **my** gym shoes in **your** locker?

These possessive pronouns stand alone in sentences: **mine, yours, his, hers, its, ours, theirs**.

> Are those gym shoes **mine** or are they **yours**?

4. Indefinite Pronouns

A pronoun that does not take the place of a particular noun is called an **indefinite pronoun**.

> **Nobody** can be right about **everything.**

Chapter 6: Pronouns That Ask and Point

1. Pronouns That Ask

An interrogative pronoun is used in a question. **What, which, who, whom**, and **whose** are interrogative pronouns. **Who** and **whom** refer to a person or persons. **Whose** is used when asking about ownership or relationship. **What** refers to places, things, and ideas. **Which** is used when there is a choice between two or more persons, places, or things.

> **What** do you see?
>
> **Who** is there?
>
> **Which** did she prefer?

2. Demonstrative Pronouns

Demonstrative pronouns point out one or more people, places, or things. These words are demonstrative pronouns: **this, that, these** and **those**.

> **These** are the funniest cartoons.
>
> Nobody laughed at **those**.

3. Relative Pronouns

A relative pronoun connects a noun or pronoun with a group of words that tells more about it. **That, which, who, whom,** and **whose** are relative pronouns.

> We found a woman **who** could give us directions.
>
> The story **that** I heard was quite different.

Chapter 7: Verb Forms

1. What Are Verbs?

A verb expresses action or being. Every sentence must have a verb.

The volcano **erupts** about once every ten years.

It **is** always a terrific surprise.

2. Action Verbs

Most verbs are action verbs. An action verb expresses physical or mental action.

They **left** in the middle of the movie.

They **disliked** its violence.

3. Linking Verbs

A linking verb tells what the subject is or seems to be. The most common linking verb is **be.**

Ralph **is** a bus driver.

He **looks** good in his uniform.

4. Present Tense Verb Forms

A verb changes form to show present and past time. The time shown by a verb is called its tense. The present tense shows action or being in the present.

The children **play** in the yard.

Most verbs have a singular and plural present tense form.

The verb in a sentence must agree with the noun or pronoun in the subject. The verb **be** has more forms than other verbs. **Be** has three present tense forms: **am, is,** and **are. Am** agrees with the pronoun **I. Is** agrees with singular nouns and the pronouns **he, she**, and **it. Are** agrees with plural nouns and the pronouns **we, you,** and **they.**

> She **is** a famous gymnast.
>
> Many people **are** her fans.
>
> I **am** a good gymnast, too.

Be has two past tense forms: **was** and **were. Was** agrees with singular noun subjects and the pronouns **he, she,** and **it. Were** agrees with plural noun subjects and the pronouns **we, you,** and **they.**

> The argument **was** noisy.
>
> Several neighbors **were** angry about it.

The singular form ends with **-s.** This form goes with singular noun subjects and with the pronoun subjects **he, she,** and **it.**

> The rabbit **jumps.**
>
> He (she, it) **jumps.**

The plural form goes with plural noun subjects and with the pronoun subjects **I, you, we,** and **they.**

> The rabbits **jump.**
>
> I (you, we, they) **jump.**

Use a singular verb with a singular indefinite pronoun.

Use a plural verb with a plural indefinite pronoun.

> Anybody **runs** faster than Michael.
>
> Many **run** faster than Michael.

Some indefinite pronouns may be singular or plural:

> all   any   most   none   some   such

Use a singular verb when you mean one person or thing.

Use a plural verb when you mean more than one person or thing.

All of the team **was** present.

All of the team (members) **were** present.

The present tense verb form that agrees with plural nouns agrees with compound subjects (two or more subjects in the sentence).

Beth Obermeyer and her daughter Kristen **hold** a record for long distance tap dancing.

Use the singular form of the verb with the title of a book or movie or the name of an organization.

The Vampires **is** a silly movie.

The United Nations **meets** in New York.

Use the singular form of the verb with an amount when you think of it as a single unit.

Three dollars **is** too much for that.

Use the plural form of the verb with an amount when you think of it as a number of separate units.

There **are** three letters for each of you.

5. Past Tense Verb Forms

Past tense verb forms show action or being in the past. Many past tense verb forms are made by adding **-d** or **-ed** to the present tense plural form.

The children **play** in the snow.

Yesterday the children **played** in the snow.

6. Irregular Past Tense Verb Forms

Some verbs do not form the past tense by adding **d** or **ed.** They form the past tense in other ways. The following words are examples of the present and past tense of irregular verbs.

eat — ate	steal — stole	burst — burst
give — gave	tear — tore	do — did
lie — lay	wear — wore	freeze — froze
come — came	take — took	speak — spoke
run — ran	know — knew	fall — fell
begin — began	grow — grew	go — went
drink — drank	blow — blew	see — saw
ring — rang	throw — threw	drive — drove
shrink — shrank	fly — flew	
swim — swam	choose — chose	

Chapter 8: Verb Phrases

1. Verb Phrases with Be

A verb phrase is made up of one or more helping verbs and a main verb. The helping verb is often a form of the verb **be.**

The man **was working** in the garden.

The main verb in a verb phrase with a form of the verb **be** is always a present participle. The present participle is formed by adding **ing** to the plural form of the verb.

2. Verb Phrases with Have

Forms of the verb **have** (have, has, had) are followed by a past participle in a verb phrase. The past participle is the main verb. It is formed by adding **d, ed, n,** or **en** to the plural form of the verb.

The group **has decided** to hold a picnic.

3. Verb Phrases with Do

Forms of the verb **do (**do, does, did) are sometimes used as a helping verb in a verb phrase. The main verb that follows **do** is always plural. The verb **do** has three main uses as a helping verb: in a question; with the word **not;** and for emphasis.

Do you **want** to eat lunch now?

I **do not want** to eat lunch now.

I **do want** to eat lunch now.

4. Verb Phrases and Not

The word **not** changes the meaning of a sentence. **Not** usually comes between the words in a verb phrase. **Not** is not part of the verb phrase.

They **are working** hard.

They **are** not **working** hard.

5. Future Tense

The future tense tells of action or being in the future. To make the future tense, use a verb phrase with **will** or **shall** and a plural verb form.

I **shall tell** you the answer.

They **will tell** me the answer.

6. Other Helping Verbs

Other helping verbs are sometimes used in verb phrases.

The helping verbs **can, could, may, might, must, should,** and **would** are followed by a plural verb form.

He **might agree** to come with us.

7. Passive Verb Phrases

Sentences in which the subject performs the action have active verbs or verb phrases.

Marie **sang** two songs.

Marie **has sung** two songs.

Sentences in which the action is performed on the subject have passive verb phrases.

Two songs **were sung** by Marie.

Chapter 9: Verbs and Sentence Patterns

1. Simple Subject and Simple Predicate

The simple subject is the subject noun or pronoun of a sentence.

The small red **car** was moving quickly down the road.

The simple predicate is the verb or verb phrase of a sentence.

The small red car **was moving** quickly down the road.

2. Direct Objects

A direct object is the noun or pronoun that receives the action of a verb. The direct object always follows an action verb. It never follows a linking verb.

We painted the **barn.**

We painted **it.**

3. Indirect Objects

An indirect object is the noun or pronoun to whom or for whom an action is done. An indirect object comes after the verb and before the direct object in a sentence. An indirect object never comes after the words **for** or **to.**

He tells **students** the same stories each year.

He tells **them** the same stories each year.

4. Object Complements

An object complement follows a direct object and refers back to it. An object complement renames or tells more about the direct object.

John thought the paintings **beautiful.**

5. Predicate Nominatives

A predicate nominative is a noun or pronoun that renames the subject noun or pronoun. The predicate nominative follows a linking verb or verb phrase.

Robert is a **teacher.**

Chapter 10: Adjectives

1. What Are Adjectives?

Adjectives tell more about a noun or pronoun. They usually tell what kind, which one, or how many.

> Those **exhausted** men have been playing tennis for **nine** hours.

> They were **determined.**

2. Adjectives Before Nouns

All adjectives can come before nouns, but the following adjectives *must* come before nouns:

a	each	most	that
an	either	neither	the
another	every	one	these
any	few	several	this
both	many	some	those

The words **a, an,** and **the** are called articles.

A is used before words that begin with consonants or a "yew" sound.

> **A** penguin cannot fly.

> Cooking is **a** useful activity.

An is used before words that begin with vowels or an unsounded **h.**

> **An** ostrich cannot fly.

> Brutus is **an** honorable man.

3. Adjectives After Linking Verbs

Adjectives can come after a form of **be** or another linking verb. Such adjectives are called predicate adjectives. A predicate adjective tells about the noun or pronoun that is the subject of the sentence.

The sky is **cloudy.**

4. Proper Adjectives

An adjective that is formed from a proper noun is a proper adjective.

An American dollar is worth less than a British pound.

The new Spielberg film is great.

5. Using Adjectives to Make Comparisons

Adjectives can be used to compare two or more people or things. When only two people or things are compared, use the form of the adjective that ends with **-er**. When more than two people or things are compared, use the form of the adjective that ends with **-est**.

Buster Keaton was **funnier** than Charlie Chaplin.

Buster Keaton was the **funniest** movie actor that ever lived.

With adjectives that have more than two syllables and with some adjectives that have two syllables, use **more** when you are comparing two people or things. Use **most** when you are comparing more than two people or things.

Buster Keaton was **more** amusing than Charlie Chaplin.

Buster Keaton was the **most** amusing movie actor who ever lived.

Use **less** to compare two people or things.

Use **least** to compare three or more people or things.

> That book was **less** interesting than the one I read yesterday.

> That book was the **least** interesting of all the books I ever read.

Use **better** to compare two people or things. Use **best** to compare more than two people or things.

> Buster Keaton was a **better** actor than Charlie Chaplin.

> Buster Keaton was the **best** movie actor who ever lived.

Use **worse** to compare two people or things. Use **worst** to compare more than two people or things.

> *The Revenge of the Killer Tomatoes* was a **worse** movie than *The Fly*.

> *The Revenge of the Killer Tomatoes* was probably the **worst** movie ever made.

6. Spelling Adjectives Correctly

Some one-syllable adjectives end with a vowel followed by a consonant. Double the final consonant before you add **er** or **est** to these adjectives.

> tan   tanner   tannest   flat   flatter   flattest

Some adjectives end with a consonant followed by **-y**.

Change the **y** to **i** before adding **er** or **est** to these adjectives.

> lazy   lazier   laziest   happy   happier   happiest

7. Exact Adjectives

Writing can be made clearer and more interesting by using exact adjectives.

The truck went up the hill.

The **old** truck went up the **big** hill.

The **rusty**, **red** truck went up the **steep**, **rocky** hill.

Chapter 11: Adverbs

1. What Are Adverbs?

An adverb tells more about a verb or verb phrase. An adverb tells how, where, when, or how many times an action takes place.

The rodeo rider **bravely** mounted the bronco **again.**

2. Adverbs That Tell More About Adjectives

Some adverbs tell more about adjectives. These adverbs tell how much, how little, and to what degree.

The room was **quite** cold.

Some adverbs that tell more about adjectives:

very	rather	extremely	exceptionally	truly
too	fairly	unusually	somewhat	especially

3. Adverbs That Tell More About Other Adverbs

Some adverbs tell more about other adverbs. They tell how much, how little, how often, and to what degree.

The people left **very** quickly.

Some adverbs that tell more about other adverbs:

very	rather	truly	exceptionally	quite
too	fairly	unusually	somewhat	especially

4. Knowing When to Use Adjectives and Adverbs

Use adjectives to tell more about nouns and pronouns.

The **proud** actor accepted the prize.

Use adverbs to tell more about verbs and verb phrases, adjectives, and adverbs.

The actor **proudly** accepted the prize.

Use the adjective **good** to tell more about a noun or pronoun.

Use the adverb **well** to tell more about a verb or verb phrase.

I just read a **good** book.

The author writes **well.**

5. Using Adverbs to Make Comparisons

Adverbs can be used to compare the actions of two or more people or things. When the actions of only two people or things are compared, use **more** or **less** before the adverb. When the actions of more than two people or things are compared, use **most** or **least** before the adverb.

Polly speaks **more** clearly than that other parrot.

Of all those parrots, Polly speaks **most** clearly.

Add **-er** to a few short adverbs to compare the actions of two people or things. Add **-est** to those same adverbs to compare the actions of more than two.

Polly can fly **higher** than that other parrot.

Of all those parrots, Polly can fly the **highest.**

The forms of the adverb **well** are **well, better,** and **best.**

Use **better** to compare the actions of two people or things.

Use **best** to compare the actions of more than two things.

That parrot behaved **better** than your pet cat.

Of all the pets in the show, the parrot behaved **best**.

Use **worse** to compare the actions of two people or things.

Use **worst** to compare the actions of more than two things.

The monkey behaved **worse** than the parrot.

Of all the pets in the show, your cat behaved **worst.**

6. Avoiding Double Negatives

A negative is a word or phrase that expresses denial
or says "no." These words are negatives:

no	no one	nowhere	barely
not	nobody	none	scarcely
never	nothing	hardly	

The negative adverb **not** can be joined to a verb. The
new word is a contraction. Some examples are:

are not: aren't	will not: won't
do not: don't	would not: wouldn't

Use only one negative word to make a sentence
mean **no** or **not**. Avoid double negatives.

No one understands how I feel.

Hardly anyone understands how I feel.

7. Exact Adverbs

Use exact adverbs to make writing clearer and more
interesting.

Jim spoke.

Jim spoke **well.**

Jim spoke **clearly** and **forcefully.**

Chapter 12: Prepositions and Prepositional Phrases

1. What Is a Preposition?

A preposition shows how a noun or pronoun is related to another word or group of words in a sentence. These are the most common prepositions:

about	below	in	to
above	beneath	into	toward
across	beside	like	under
after	between	of	until
against	beyond	off	up
along	by	on	upon
among	down	over	with
around	during	past	within
at	except	since	without
before	for	through	
behind	from	throughout	

The cars moved **across** the bridge.

2. What Is a Prepositional Phrase?

A preposition and the noun or pronoun that follows it form a prepositional phrase. If there are other words between the preposition and the noun or pronoun, these words are part of the prepositional phrase.

A new record for sit-ups was set **by Dr. David G. Jones.**

His family and friends were proud **of him.**

3. Pronouns in Prepositional Phrases

Use these personal pronouns in prepositional phrases: **me, you, him, her, it, us, them.**

The other presents **for her** are still on the table.

4. Prepositional Phrases in the Subject

Sometimes a prepositional phrase comes after the main noun in the subject. The prepositional phrase is a part of the subject. The verb or verb phrase agrees with the main noun or pronoun. The verb does not have to agree with the noun or pronoun in the prepositional phrase.

One of the women **is** driving the bus.

The books on the shelf **are** math books.

5. Using Prepositions Correctly

Use **between** when you refer to two people or things.

The band leader was standing **between** the drummer and the pianist.

Use **among** when you refer to more than two people or things.

The band leader was standing **among** all the musicians.

The preposition **beside** means "next to."

The oak trees grew **beside** the creek.

The preposition **besides** means "in addition to" or "except."

Besides ice cream, they ate cake and cookies.

Chapter 13: Other Phrases

1. Appositive Nouns and Appositive Phrases

An appositive noun directly follows a pronoun or another noun and tells more about it or renames it.

That woman, **Ms. Ellison**, spoke to our club.

An appositive phrase contains an appositive noun. An appositive phrase is placed next to a noun or pronoun to tell more about it or to rename it.

Ms. Ellison, **the mayor of River City**, spoke to our club.

2. Participial Phrases

A participial phrase begins with either a present participle, such as **sitting**, or a past participle, such as **seated.**

A participial phrase gives more information about a noun or pronoun.

Sitting comfortably, my grandfather reached for the phone.

Seated near the door, he got up when the bell rang.

3. Gerunds and Gerund Phrases

A gerund is a present participle, a verb that ends in **-ing**. It is always used as a noun.

Fishing is my aunt's favorite sport.

My uncle thinks **fishing** is a bore.

A gerund phrase begins with a gerund. The other words in the phrase tell more about the gerund. A gerund phrase is used as a noun.

Fishing in the surf can tire you quickly.

---

4. Infinitives and Infinitive Phrases

An infinitive consists of the word **to** and the plural form of a verb such as **go** or **study.** An infinitive phrase begins with an infinitive. Other words in the phrase tell more about the infinitive. Infinitive phrases can be used as nouns.

Jed decided **to study** hard.

To pass the test was his goal.

Chapter 14: Clauses and Conjunctions

---

1. What Is a Coordinating Conjunction?

A coordinating conjunction joins two words, groups of words, or sentences. The coordinating conjunctions are **and, but, or, nor, for, so,** and **yet.**

Many people have driven across the country, **but** these men did it the hard way.

Charles Creighton **and** James Hargis drove across the country **and** back again.

They never stopped the engine **or** took the car out of reverse gear.

2. What Is a Compound Sentence?

A simple sentence has one subject and one predicate. A compound sentence consists of two simple sentences joined by **and, but,** or **or**. A compound sentence has at least two subjects and two predicates.

Ed went skiing, **but** Kay went ice skating.

Both sentences in a compound sentence are independent clauses. A clause is a group of words with a subject and predicate. An independent clause can stand alone as a complete sentence.

3. Commas in Compound Sentences

Use a comma before the coordinating conjunction in a compound sentence.

Julie went to the movies, **but** Jack stayed home.

4. Using Coordinating Conjunctions to Combine Sentences

You can combine two sentences by using a coordinating conjunction and a comma.

You can watch TV now.

You can eat dinner.

You can watch TV now, **or** you can eat dinner.

5. What Are Subordinating Conjunctions?

A subordinating conjunction is a word or group of words that introduces a dependent clause. A dependent clause cannot stand alone as a complete sentence.

John sat at his desk **until he finished the exam.**

These are the most common subordinating conjunctions:

after	because	so that	whenever
although	before	than	where
as	if	though	wherever
as if	in order that	unless	whether
as long as	provided that	until	while
as though	since	when	

6. Adverb Clauses in Complex Sentences

A complex sentence consists of an independent clause (which can stand alone) and a dependent clause (which cannot stand alone). One kind of dependent clause is an adverb clause. It begins with a subordinating conjunction.

An adverb clause is used as an adverb in a sentence. It tells more about a verb and answers the question **how, why, where,** or **when.**

Otto E. Funk played his violin **while he walked from New York City to San Francisco.**

independent clause: Otto E. Funk played his violin

dependent clause: while he walked from New York City to San Francisco

subordinating conjunction: while

When he finished his trip, both his hands and feet were tired.

independent clause: both his hands and feet were tired

dependent clause: when he finished his trip

subordinating conjunction: when

7. Commas in Complex Sentences

Put a comma after the dependent clause if it comes before the independent clause.

When he was named hockey's most valuable player, Wayne Gretsky was only 18 years old.

8. Using Subordinating Conjunctions to Combine Sentences

You can combine two sentences by using a subordinating conjunction.

Jenny bought the black dress.

It was on sale.

Jenny bought the black dress **because** it was on sale.

Because it was on sale, Jenny bought the black dress.

Chapter 15: Adjective Clauses and Noun Clauses

1. What Is an Adjective Clause?

An adjective clause is a dependent clause that acts as an adjective in a sentence. An adjective clause tells more about a noun or a pronoun. Adjective clauses begin with these words: **who, which, that, whom, whose, where, when.**

The class enjoyed the music **that you played.**

2. Commas with Adjective Clauses

Adjective clauses that are essential to the meaning of a sentence are called **restrictive adjective clauses.**

Musicians **who can read music** get the best jobs.

Adjective clauses that are not essential to the meaning of a sentence are called **nonrestrictive adjective clauses.** Use a comma before and after each nonrestrictive adjective clause.

Marty, **who can read music**, works in Ted's band.

3. Using Adjective Clauses to Combine Sentences

You can combine two sentences by using an adjective clause.

Linda read a book.

The book was written by Mark Twain.

Linda read a book **that was written by Mark Twain.**

4. What Is a Noun Clause?

A noun clause is a dependent clause that is used as a noun in a sentence. A noun clause can begin with one of these words:

how	whatever	which	whose
that	when	who	why
what	where	whoever	whomever

Whoever cooked dinner left the kitchen a mess.

How we will get it cleaned is a problem.

Index